Incidents From a Shelter
(The Season of the Larva)

By

Karen Maxwell

ISBN: 1-4033-0099-2

This book is printed on acid free paper.

1stBooks - rev. 05/09/02

This book is dedicated to all women all over the world who live on the fringe of society. To the women who are brave enough to exist in a dimension other than mainstream society. I wrote this book in praise of these souls who take the risk of living differently from the way the rest of the world wants them to. With love and respect this book is for all our mothers, sisters, friends and neighbors.

-K. Maxwell

Introduction

A homeless woman sitting on a bench, alone, was the first thing I noticed when I came to the shelter for the first time. I looked a little further and there were more homeless women sitting on a few benches. The benches were in this large, wide hall with elegant chandeliers, fine panel woodwork and hard wood floors. The women looked like motionless birds. Heads, nicely rounded from scarves and hats. Their forms curved, swollen, and quiet. Their legs had varicosity's. These were not youngsters. There was not a lot of vitality in this corridor of tenants where the air moved from open fire doors and fans. In my first few steps into the shelter, as I looked into their faces, I was too eager to smile. I was happy to be there, yet embarrassed to look at them. They looked tired and lost and I didn't want them to know that I could see this in them. More than anything, I didn't want to intrude into their lives. Who was I to do that? I didn't mean anything to them. I was beginning a new job and what did they care? I also couldn't be sure that I was not projecting my feelings onto them. Maybe I was the one who was tired and scared.

Nothing I had done in life had prepared me for this work, in as much as everything I had done had prepared me for it. I was a writer when I was hired as a manager at the shelter so the flow of documenting shelter stories came easily and naturally to me. My mother was a social worker before it became popular to get degrees and to earn a living doing so. While she didn't earn a degree to be kind and helpful to others, it is something she did in her life and I learned by her example. I have a vivid memory of watching my mother take bags of groceries to a welfare family that lived down the street from us in Bayshore, Long Island.

They were in need and without question she was going to help.

In the beginning I was cautious. I had heard all the stories of these kind of women: homeless women. Friends told me to "be careful in there." They have diseases, and "you'll catch something." Indeed, I would be careful. I would look over my shoulder and I would never turn my back on "one of them." When this job was offered to me I wanted it more than anything. I felt an immediate compassion for the homeless on the streets. The magic started to work quite quickly. They were just like me. Like my family. They were women, after all, and I loved women, understood them. I was close to my mother and my grandmothers were always of interest to me. I was part of their lives until they died one at eighty-eight, and the other at ninety-four-years-old.

The women I am profiling here are from different places in the world. In likeness, they fight and laugh. They talk incessantly and sleep in the dorms together. Total strangers at first that bond because of experience and need. Would I not get close to one or more of them if I were homeless and in a shelter? Wouldn't you adapt and find at least one person that you had something in common with? Likeness in genetics? Ages? And even addictions.

A few of these women once had careers, but trauma and mental illness can wreck havoc with the most stable of souls. One of our women was a teacher of literature. We found out that she had also lost a child to death at an early age. By the time our paths crossed she was in full bloom psychosis.

Sometimes the women live at the shelter for a very long time, and because of fear, mental illness, dependency, obsessive behaviors, and loneliness they don't want to leave and are unable to leave. A lot of them never learned how to take care of themselves. The mentally ill frequently live with their families, without treatment, until either a family throws them out or dies. There was one woman who lived with her sister, and her sister's husband. When the sister died, the brother in law threw the woman out into the street.

If they are substance abusing they have probably been doing so for most of their lives. This early dependency knocked them out of the candidacy list for education or a solid work history. Successes in either area could have contributed to helping the women feeling better about themselves.

What's also amazing is how other workers from city agencies don't have a clue to what has happened to these women. I had some man come from the city fire department and he wanted to know about the women and how they ended up here. He used words like lazy, and losing ones home from a fire or flood, or the death of their husband. In the country where he came from, monsoon rains would cause catastrophic housing problems. These are not women from his part of the world, yet he needed to compartmentalize them according to his experience for his need only.

This shelter helps women without prejudice. We shelter, feed, and clothe them when they arrive. Their social workers have the job of trying to right some of the wrongs that have been done to these women. So many layers of disharmony from mental illness, family rage, unloving experiences and then whack, they are with us. We unravel horror stories and reinforce that we will care for them.

There is a culture born here of people who live like they are either in a large family, or in jail. They fight with each other and take care of each other. It is hard for the staff not to "adopt" some of them and not feel protective of them. These are women 45 years and older who are not in great health, a few are quite fragile. Staff tell each other that they would never let their mother's end up like this. And they probably won't, but their hearts are really tender for these women who have supposedly very little in their lives. We give them parties for every occasion, provide personal amenities like shampoo, soap, lotion, powder, diapers and sanitary napkins. We constantly clean the place after them which may not be the best thing. Ideally, they need to be responsible for the mess they make. But who is going to change an eighty-year-old. We have one lady who is that old and a difficult client to reach. Patsy, we call her for Patricia, likes it that way, and she drags many pieces of fabric from all over the city back to the area around her bed. She collects doll clothes and washes them in the washing machines. These tiny, articles of clothes cause a fight when someone is waiting to wash their clothes. But who is to say what is more important? There was once an onion stuck in her sneaker and when staff were walking around she tried to hide it. Now what was she going to do with the onion? Her worker put it in the refrigerator for her to use at later date but was that onion a symbol of taking care of herself? Or for medicinal purposes? She wouldn't tell us.

There is another woman who wraps up boxes of little cereal in toilet paper and then in plastic bags with rubber bands. She also wraps up wash cloths that are wet! Fruit, that bring many larva and flies, and dirty underwear the same way. Occasionally, we just throw the stuff away. The Department of Homeless Services allows us to inspect the women's belongings following certain procedures. Mostly, we do it when bags are oversized and the smell is overwhelming. As we have many things to look out for frequently in one breath, we are expected to also comply with the Fire Department and the Department of Health.

We have learned to put the alcoholics and bed wetters close to the bathroom. Each woman has her own story. Each has different needs.

We have seen big strong sons come and ask their aging and poor mothers for money. We have seen the mothers give the money to their sons. One strategy to get them a little antsy and to help them to think independently, is to move their sleeping locations. This is a shelter intended as a stop off place to live while she waits for permanent housing to come through. It is for transient purposes only. Some of the women get accustomed to the institutional life. A few are terrified to live on their own. Afraid if they get sick, no one will be there. That they could be found dead on the floor of their apartment is the worst thing imaginable to them. Their fears, phobias and social diseases keep them from living.

I wrote this book as a poet who got to swim with her subject every day.

In closing, I just want to mention a contractor I met one day who was visiting the shelter as he was going to provide our shelter with fire inspections. All he kept saying was how lucky he was that he had his life and that he would never have to live like this because he had family. After he left I tried numerous times to get him on the phone so we could sign the contract papers, but he wouldn't talk to me. His behavior spoke volumes for the general population and how they view the homeless.

Prologue

Joilee swims down the hallway. Her volume croons into the dim antique sconces. Arthritic hands bend catching dust that falls onto her memory. Walk two steps along and she knows that she is in a woman's shelter with one-hundred-and-eighteen other roommates. Three, four, five, and she is at home with her young sons running into another room to get away from her wife-beating husband. Joilee smells bad. The staff don't inhale but breath through their mouths when they are near her. She wears a terrycloth robe, sandals, and pink plastic earrings with silver bulbs in the center. In the reflection of the bulb one can see the other women. On her ears is a scope of the women in this shelter, an opportunity to watch them without them knowing. Irish, African, Puerto Rican, Dominican, American women. The hall dangles from Joilees ears, convexing the women into bulbous faces, and no feet. Her mind grabs her social worker's words. She looks into her eyes, she is working very hard this afternoon. She will try again to deliver her from the demons that torment her. The earrings, bathrobe, and language are all talking at one time. She wears lipstick beyond her lip lines. Her black hair is greasy and straight. A few gray hairs stand alone. Sticking out, hard, and dull, like death. She's almost an exotic beauty. There are remnants of that life in her from time to time. She never talks about her sons to her worker and when she does, an attempt is made to get in to her head. Her face drops downward and she wraps the crooked fingers on her left hand around the fingers on her right. Youth and old age stare at the social worker in this shelter. The veil of her innocence has fallen away under the commands of these sisters whom she chooses to love and accept exactly as they are. The more the worker becomes involved in this women's homeless shelter the less she can remember who she was before she got here.

BRUISES

Karen Maxwell

Monday September 13, 1999

Sigrid's hands are blue and icy. White bubbly drool and sneezes intertwine and snake down her chin. She moves like a puck in a pinball game. *Bing, bing* when she hits into someone, bouncing off, *bing, bing*. Overwhelmed by her own movements *bing*, each direction she takes is too much for her and she turns fast drunk at 11 AM and loving the self torment. Loving the high, staying in the chaos in the feeling of the light-headedness and the mind out there. Out there. Where?

Thomasina stands in the doorway, waiting for the elevator to come. She has a plastic package with socks: new socks for her old feet. She is three and a half feet tall and there is a lump on her head. Someone flatters her and she gets angry because she knows they are lying to her. She is ugly, but not stupid. "You insult me when you talk to me like that. Please don't do it," she says. "Go help that poor soul who's always drunk. Take care of her and leave me alone."

Herminia hears no one. The banter, and the air charged with soul potential, has nothing to do with her. So she laughs at her own thoughts while sitting on a bench by the elevator with the Holy Bible opened. She runs her finger under the prayer words, reciting the messages of God the Father. She feels safe as He holds her in the palm of His hands; she brings Him to her mind, into her heart. Now it's Jesus whom she abandons herself for. Her once active loins are quieted. The old power of hair-curling orgasms has surrendered the pulse to Him. Herminia writes letters and takes notes that she keeps in spiral notebooks. They are jammed into her locker that she is unable to close. There is a banal grin on her face. She looks over at Sigrid who is still *bing, binging* across the room. Sigrid lights up and breathes in the smoke. Her extremities are moistened from body lotion.

Sigrid was brought back from the hospital last night and now she is washing her clothes during a hectic morning in the shelter. She chain smokes to catch her youth. She drinks to forget that she is alive. She was found on the sidewalk, her body contorted into the iron fence around the armory. The empty bottle of vodka balanced itself on her hip. It was illuminated in the sun like a full-page advertisement in the *New York Times*. A social worker and a manager stayed on the sidewalk and stood over Sigrid, calling her name. This is Sigrid's memory of a good time. Getting slam down drunk, plastered, and having a rescue team save her. The dance is over for Sigrid, but she doesn't know it. Her frosty spit is an infection in her upper respiratory area, yet because she doesn't want to be hospitalized, no one can force her to be examined. EMS is called anyway and shortly after they arrive, they peel her bluish body off the ground. She opens her eyes when her name is called. When she sobers up she grieves the first time she got drunk in the South when she was a tiny princess desired by the prominent princes in all of Dade County.

Southern girls, fifty years ago, were born to be beauties. Every nuance and manner curtailed and groomed to peak the true gentleman's heart. Sigrid's eyes, still pointed in the violet direction, but every time she opened them with her head against the railing, she flashed the memory of that back to the staff. They would not forget her image any time soon, as the vision of the lost Southern girl who was metaphorically grounded in her time.

Today Sigrid is wearing white anklet socks, a practical house dress with tiny flowers on it, and her face has been washed so it shines like the vodka bottle in yesterday's sun. Sigrid's blood lies down, too, in the lower depths of her form, coagulating, stagnating beneath cobalt fingertips. Sigrid's calling in a moment was to hem lines, scotch & soda, plantation sized shopping malls, and Virginia Slims.

But here at the shelter, where the halls are lit by fluorescent lights and the pine doors need help staying closed, social workers are assigned to at least nine other women: The lost-and-found bodies of aged, intoxicated, splotched, and shoeless women of New York City. English, Spanish, African American, Dominican, Costa Rican, Polish, Swedish, from the South Bronx, or six blocks away, it doesn't matter where they came from, when they get here it's either the beginning or the end of the road. They sit and wait for time to pile on, one minute, two minutes, five minutes before the hour, five minutes after the hour. Stagnant breathing in the core of the shelter, full legs crossed at the ankles. Empty lives that look to fill their bellies with crackers and jelly. Ironic statements of gloom, laughing at each other's misery, of which they cannot really see. Clouds surround them. No one exists except them, except who they are. But the workers care about them; at times they love them. They want to go back and mend their lives: To take them away from their abuse, to get them help for their mental illnesses thirty years ago, when they were told they were "bad," or "crazy." Every word they say to each client has been chosen for impact. Social workers need to get maximum mileage for their sessions with their clients. They don't have much time to help them, as most are at the end of their lives. Poor eating habits and no medical attention when it was needed. This is how they get the women. Society's Grandmother cast off into the sunset of a New York City shelter.

#   #   #

At this morning's community meeting everyone is privileged to meet, the newest arrival and, the shelter's very own dermatologist. It becomes helter, shelter for Theresa.

"I'm Dr. Beatrice Moore-Delaney, and I have been a dermatologist for twenty-five years." Dr. Moore-Delaney stands up and waves to everyone with a hanky. She is a sweet, baby-doll-faced woman with a long net filled with hair that goes across her shoulders and down her back. She wears a white belt from a skirt wrapped around her hair and across the top of her head. She arrived two days ago, then came to this meeting on this day to express her gratitude and to say how happy she is that she is here. "I met," she said, "fourteen of my old friends right here in this shelter. I just can't believe it! And don't you know, they are telling me the rules. I am just so happy to be here and I want ya all to know this. That I am so happy to make your acquaintance."

The nurse whispered something about her crash and that when it happens we will be seeing the other side of Miss overjoyed-I'm-so-happy-I'm-here-I-just-met-fourteen-of-my-old-friends-crazy-lady.

Her bed is located in the big dorm on the upper floor where most of the beds are kept. She has decided to organize her personal items in used cardboard boxes. Sadie stands up and tries to tell her that the shelter doesn't allow the women to keep cardboard boxes in one's locker or around one's bed because they can catch fire quickly. She doesn't look happy or very agreeable when she is told this. Maybe the crash is starting a little bit already. She doesn't realize it but when the cleanup crew discover the boxes tomorrow they will throw the damn things into the garbage and then the next time she will not even think about collecting her precious items in those boxes, unless she is just obstinate. Then the workers will have to deal with that, in addition to her mental deficits.

Sara smothers her face into her jacket. Laughing first, then taking refuge in the dankness of her clothes. The meeting won't be adjourned until at least one half hour has passed. In the corner of the room, leaning against the wall, she mumbles about the smell of a man's semen. Her body takes on the form of a man. She remembers getting bathed in the swirl of men before she was old enough to understand the sexual part of herself. Her consciousness has been anointed in the warm spirit of an old man's penis. He is now her Lord. Sara takes tiny cups of bleach to kill the unseen germs. She drags her cart of books and blouses in and out of doorways, a beige cardigan folded over her arm. Sara cuts her hair completely off until the scalp is showing. No one can penetrate her now without her seeing them first. The social workers signal to each other with their eyes. They glance in Sara's direction. If she continues one of them will get up and talk to her to stop her from getting out of control.

Toward the end of the meeting they ask for good news. Frances Licht, one of the other clients, raises her hand. "I am leaving the shelter the end of this week because I have found housing." The group clap, and smile, at her.

Theresa walks over to the coffee table. She whispers loudly, and in monotone: "They all got issues. That's the phrase they be saying all over this place lately. She got issues; he got issues. All God's children got issues. Well, why the hell not! These mother fuckers who is workin' here be treatin' us like we the only damn persons on the mother fuckin' face of the mother fuckin' earth with issues. Hell, goddamnit, we all got issues. Even God got issues for creating us when you think about it. Look at what he done did to the whole wide world." Theresa looks straight ahead or downward. She takes a stirrer, and sips her coffee.

She reaches for the milk: "We used to be singin' that in church when I was so young as a girl, about God and that

He had the whole world in His hands. I be sittin' up at the front pew thinkin' all sorts of ungodly things like about the minister and if he still be doin' it to his wife. Now I wasn't supposed to be thinkin' like that as I was a little girl an' all an' daddy for sure he would take me to the woods for a lickin' if'n he knew how I wasn't all that sugar stuff after all."

Two social workers, Dennis and Mary, approach her. "Do you want to stay for the meeting?" Mary asks. Theresa gets quiet. She rocks from foot to foot, she holds the coffee with one hand, adjusts her sweater around her shoulder with the other.

"Ms. Dr. Moore-Delaney is interrupting my childhood this time, cause now she wants the rest of the room to know how she be usen' the same cup for her bleach that she use for her morning coffee. She just want us to think she is such a good ol' girl, a doctor girl. Somebody once tol' her that she had pretty skin so she decide now to pretend that she a skin doctor. But nobody really care what she came from or where the hell she been, she here now with the rest of us. She be misfittin' her pretty little skinned self all around this damn shelter like she a real doctor, but we knows enough by now just to feel sorry for her."

"You'll have to leave the meeting if you can't be quiet, Theresa," Dennis says.

Theresa has a void expression on her face. "Somedays I feel so sick and tired of this place and this social worker be at me every time I starts to get some rest, that I wants to do anything that I can to get on up outta' here. Can't gets no rest here with all the men runnin' around all night tryin' to rape the women's. I watch them comn' by the beds at night, lookin' for the right one. They all be pullin' the blankets on up over their heads and the women too scared to say anythin'. I was meetin' with Ms. Joanne the other day and she be tryin' to pull all sorts of things about my family outta me. That ain't any of her business what my family be like. I has a fine family and they be good folk. What she and that director need to be doin' is takin' care of the soldiers and the firemen who be roamin' the halls, and not worryin' about my family. I just don't wants to answer to no girl who wear those pants all the time. Those farmer lookin' pants like she be makin' fun o' hard workin' folks by wearin' those clothes. Ms. Joanne need to be wearin' skirts like a lady."

The meeting quiets while waiting for Theresa to leave the room. Frances's graduation is now old news. Everyone is watching Theresa leave. The meeting is adjourned.

Each sheltered woman here is different, like having children and loving them all, yet knowing that they don't need to get the same things. The shelter loves each woman like a mother loving her children.

Theresa with her small, fine hands. Sculptured at the wrist into smooth and movable joints of creation. Her social worker, Joanne, has discovered so many things about her. The way she reaches for things with all four fingers, curling them into the cupped palm of her hand. The thumb sticks out then locks around the fingers when the grab is done. Say hello to Theresa? She salutes you back with one pointed finger. From the side of her face while looking forward she will see you. She waves not moving her mouth; her inability to smile back is always present.

Today she wears a different, oversized kelly green shirt that covers her plum, colored dress. Her big, brown eyes, freeze when you look at her one second too long. Her head is covered in black, polyester fabric, cut from a previous dress or shirt, tailored to seclude her highest place.

She roams the basement in the night when most are sleeping. Those who are jolted awake, or others like Chynna Maryanne who lies still waiting for the babies to

9

come along, keep away from each other in the witching hours.

Mandy

Mandy, snaps up and awake at night when she hears beds move and steel springs squeak. Tired female bodies mesh into poorly ventilated rooms: Strangers in the flesh, sisters in their consciousness.

Mandy, a little lady of Puerto Rican and German descent, dazzles and jewels herself each day with colors, and she nods out from drugs while listening to a high powered Walkman. Every other tooth in her mouth is missing but she still chews gum, eats candy, sucks on straws that are slanted into coca cola cans. Blue tips tapping from her finger nails, they are her pride and folly. Fanning her nails out in front of her face, fat and happy, she sings along with the radio plugged into her ears. At forty-nine years old, her ankles swell, her feet are cranked with arthritis. "Life," she says "is tough."

Theresa watches Mandy, the colorful lady who has Spanish features and blond hair. Fake rubies and emeralds dangle from the tight ringlet curls in her thin, light hair. Theresa has wondered out loud what it must feel like to be so light in color, yet so heavy. She puts her hand to her chin, scathing the small hairs that dot the area. Not feeling like a man, but managing the manliness on her changing body.

Mandy smiles every time she sees people that she knows. She wants the hot cocoa from the reception desk. She asks politely for donated cookies when they are enroute to a socialwork group. Mandy piles her plate up high at most meals. Sometimes she nods out over dinner. Especially when it has been two days since she has slept. It's not only coffee and cranky beds that keep her awake, but the unmerciful, taxing life of using drugs.

Mandy often talks about the life she once lived in Jamaica, New York. She grew up around the area where the E and F trains connect to the Long Island busses that go slightly past the Queens and Nassau County boarder onto Long Island. Mandy talks about Long Island as a place where she wanted to go but couldn't ever manage to. She hung out around the bus depo that had a tunnel connection between 166th and 167th Streets. That's where she learned about drugs and men. The tunnel became home to Mandy on a cold night when the friction of lighted matches and hot dicks beckoned her for attention. She was able to manage both. Unlike Theresa, who could only feel warmth from a song, or from hours of dreaming behind the walls in her Daddy's well-swatted Georgian house, Mandy was from the street. She could get high and be comfortable nodding out anywhere. Theresa secured herself to darkened hallways and distant military men. Theresa, who could hardly look people in the face and would run to the corners of darkened rooms to cough.

Living is hard for Mandy, but it is harder for her to take care of herself. Mandy gets dressed each day to leave the mother shelter to get high. Glitzly dressed, she wanders onto the trains that lead her back to the streets where nurturing is satisfied in the puff of a crack pipe. Her family dried out after twenty-five years of supporting the non supporting junkie that they once loved. She stays close to Monique, who is African American and from North Carolina, who smokes and puffs too.

They pine for Frankie and whatever strength is left in her track-ridden arms. Frankie went to live with her son, but was taken to jail for shoplifting. They haven't heard from her since, but still they long for the good old days of hanging out and smoking crack in Frankie's apartment in Bed Stuy, Brooklyn. Frankie once told a manager: "I'm street, and I know I'm street. But these new folks you have around here are stealing from everyone." While she was talking, she nodded like a junkie and fluttered her eyelids in an attempt to keep awake. She held onto a cigarette the whole time. The manager kept looking at Frankie and thinking how pretty she was, how naturally beautiful her face was. But it wasn't enough to keep Frankie away from drugs. Then she gets a hit, a sweet hit of her smoke, and the world is good, all are welcome into her home!

Theresa is huddling against the bench in the third-floor hallway. She whisks past the old lady, Celia, who lives like a behemoth whale, taking up the energy by the staircase, Theresa's favorite place. Celia in her bold, antagonistic arrogance, sits, sleeps, and eats on the same plastic couch every day. Her bottom is wide like an umbrella. She appears to have no chest. Her neck is small. Her head sits like an aged pea on top of the world tight, small, and lethal. She lines up her fruits in a row on the back of the couch. The only time Celia leaves the building is when there is a fire drill and she is forced to. Everyone has been baptized into Celia's arena of name calling. Most have been called "mother fuckers" by her when they get too close to her space. The vending machines are next to her couch. She drops coins into the slots for soda and candy. Celia falls asleep with the creamy part of a Milky Way on her teeth.

Tuesday, September 14, 1999

Frances will be leaving the shelter in a few days, and her definitions are changing. The fine emotions that run under her skin have become softer. The head is held higher. She sits, today, on a bench in a hall outside the bedroom area where she sleeps. She and Joanne see each other and smile. At times, the rules between she and Joanne have been stretched. They often relate as women together. Even though Frances is twenty years older than Joanne, and they are not related, they are like mother, like child, like sister.

Joanne went over and sat on the bench that is more like a pew in a church with Frances. It was nearing lunch time and Joanne suggested that they meet after lunch today at one o'clock. Frances looked at Joanne and the smile began in her eyes, "You're always looking out for me first," Frances said.

The shelter was still warm from the summer months, the bricks of the building still hot from the ferocious New York City sun. The fans had been slanted upward to counter the rising heat. "Would you prefer to sit outside? Or we can stay here," Joanne said. They had done this before. To sit outside, sometimes among the bustle, gives a sense of rhythm and humanness to their sessions. It's like saying to her "there is life out there and you need to go and live in it." She said she would, so by one 'o'clock they were each grabbing chairs and taking the elevator to the ground level.

Once outside, they sighed with relief. The city air, the struggling weeds in the cracks of the sidewalks, and the dog walkers added humor to their discussions. They were cooler on the outside. A housekeeper walked past them with two matching white poodles. Joanne tried to figure out her own feelings and what part of the session was for her.

She was worried that Frances would still need her and that she wouldn't be there.

"You have your notebook?" Joanne asked, knowing that the book is filled with source information for her. She thought about how she used to ask Frances if she made "those phone calls yet." Always, the replanting of ideas and then the follow up and the "did you?" stuff. They have spent weeks getting ready for the send off. The bon voyage. Joanne is fearful that Frances *will* need her; Joanne is fearful that Frances *will not* need her.

Joanne's experiences at the shelter prepare her for her lovers, and her yet-to-be-born children. She now see's her mother, and grandmothers with a different set of eyes. How women are all so interconnected is apparent to her since her work with the women at the shelter.

"So what's going on?" Joanne asks. "Are you feeling okay today about the changes?" Tried and true, social worker catch words, but damn if they don't still work.

"Yes, yes, everything is in its place. I feel so blessed," Frances says. "Everyone at the shelter has been so wonderful and helpful to me."

"We have some household items that you can take to the SRO, like cleaning supplies and linens, to start you off."

"Yes, of course. I'll take them"

"You know that you can call me if anything comes up again for you."

Frances smiles at Joanne. They both know that she won't. Frances, who taught children in the New York City public school system and wrote poetry in her spare time, has been given a second chance at her independence. Joanne has tried to get her to talk about her feelings about staying at the shelter. She thought about the locker she was assigned, along with the bed that was situated in a room filled with strangers. How she was limited in the amount of things she could have: Two bags allowed to be kept on top of the bed

15

during the day. A hard rule to enforce. So many women with so much hoarding. Frances was always compliant. And in Joanne's examination of the feelings that they both have, she recalled the first day Frances came here. How she looked like a regular person, and in fact was. That she had that real "fish out of water" look to her more than most. She smelled a bit of alcohol, the hours-old ferment smell that's unmistakable on a body. And so, the first time Joanne met Frances she had to ask if she abused alcohol. Her response was "no" that she was so distressed from the assessment shelter, north of the city, that she went out with another woman from there and the other woman drank, "so I did, too."

"So what happened? How did you lose your home?"

"I lost my job because I was sick. I couldn't work anymore. I have severe back trauma from an accident when I was a kid and it just got worse after I had my daughter."

Her daughter apparently lives in California and Frances didn't want to bother her or worry her, so she decided, after her eviction and no money, to see what the city could do for her. She had anticipated a dungeon. She called Joanne a healer and said that she doesn't realize the important work that she does.

During their first few meetings she presented like a disorganized, flaky individual. Not psychotic or delusional, but a little scattered. Not so unusual in any individual, but Joanne kept wondering why she didn't go to welfare to catch herself before the eviction. She never gave a straight answer on that. Maybe that is the dependent part to her personality. Perhaps it comes into focus during different times in her life. But Joanne couldn't be sure.

The shelter is like a desert today. Barren, dry ladies, two of them are sick with diarrhea. One is down with a virus. The other is very old and frail. Her insides are sandy from her bowels working and working. Theresa watches the old lady without staring this time. She is absorbing the sickness from her own private valley. The old lady stands up and a flood of feces runs out of her down onto the floor, all over her clothes until she falls down into the mess. It takes eight staff to get the room where the old lady sleeps back to order. This includes the director and the nurse practitioner. No one knows what she is sick from, but they silently wonder if a virus would have passed by now. This older lady would never see a doctor and never go for treatment for her stomach that was always sensitive to foods. Now she could be in a state of cancer that is too far gone for anyone to do anything for. The nurse calls EMS to come for her, as she needs treatment that the shelter cannot give. She is weak. The fluids start to completely abandon her body. The old lady gets strapped to a wheel chair by the EMS workers and then wheeled out of the building and driven in an ambulance to the hospital. She had an aide gather her bags so she could take them with her. Some of them are layered inside of ten bags with rubber bands tied around them. Her hair sticks straight up like tiny, gray wires. Staff know they will not see her again, as now, after the hospital, the old lady will go to a nursing home for the final days of her life. The shelter was her home. The place where she watched one-hundred-and-nineteen of her sisters live their lives. Where she ate and slept, where women took care of her like they were all her mother. Where she could wind rubber bands around her plastic bags filled with cereal boxes and wet wash cloths.

The voices in the older lady's head want her to walk. They tell her that her mother wants her home. She yells at the EMS workers to take her home, her mother needs her to set the table, her dead sister's body is in the garbage can and why don't they do something to take her out. Her screams get louder and her skin tightens up around her eyes. Her eyes are tinted with blue and green, yet they are foggy and cloudy.

Dennis, the social worker, wants her to calm down. "It's going to be okay," he tells her as the wheel chair is tilted backward. She grabs the chair like she is going to fall to the floor. The legs of her sister bend over the garbage can. She sees the motionless sister again in the basement, lying under the bench: dead. No one does anything. Don't tell her that the dead body isn't there. It is! Like you are where you are, it is, too. She wants to take her dead sister with her and make her live again. But no one listens to her, instead she is wheeled out into the air in New York City, and for one last time she looks at the armory building like it is a blanket for her death. There is nothing the staff can do for her.

Theresa has now lost her bookend on the third floor. The two old ladies were like standing posts, most days, holding up the boundaries for the ladies. Their chairs positioned at different staircase beginning points, they watched the shelter's soul roam and breathe for years.

Theresa looks strong against the older lady. They never spoke to each other, yet understood where each one lived. Theresa holds court to the staircase in the back, where the soldiers walk with guns and smoke cigars. The older lady has now left the front staircase vacant for a new watch person.

Theresa, now calm and acting like a human secret, has returned to her staircase. Theresa has told Joanne many times that these halls in the armory speak with soldiers, voices from 1875. The soldiers walk in and out of the rooms chatting away, two at a time, showing each other important papers, like maps. To them, she says, this is a modern fortress with hand-carved wood paneling and finely crafted wall paper. The confederate flag is clean and without rips in it. The cannons are new and untarnished.

There are no women in this place in 1875, except for an occasional visitor like a mother or sister, or a woman who has been brought in for their pleasure. Then they disappear as quickly as they came and a more modern military person of 1999 appears with camouflage uniform and rolled-up sleeves. Sometimes she says that she can see ghosts in full military dress walking around in the rooms that have ceilings two stories high.

Her full name is Teresa Mills. She is a sheltered homeless woman who lives in this great armory that takes up one square block in New York City. Sometimes the staff call her *Staircase Theresa* because, instead of sitting with the other one-hundred-and-nineteen women in the shelter, she hides out in the staircases or closets or behind the doors. They don't call her *Staircase Theresa* to her face. She says that she hears and sees a lot of things that she doesn't admit to. The social workers and the psychiatrists have diagnosed her with paranoid schizrophenia. She laughs and says that she knows that she is, but that she also knows that this illness has given her other abilities and talents. She says she can see through people and knows what they are thinking. She doesn't believe that most of the people here are not out to get her or to do her any harm. But a few are, and it is because of them that she stays away from the groups and meals in the large dining room. She wears dark colors to camouflage herself, much like the soldiers did, and still do, for protection. Why, then, are they not referred to as paranoid also? she asks.

She eats her meals behind the doors. She has no outside music or entertainment: Life here in this shelter is entertaining enough.

Interestingly, she knows that she is not *well* by comparison to the rest of the world. She can no longer work, outside of house work, and she has never done anything else because of the voices in her head. The voices

19

tell her what to do and when to do it. When they start, it's like having many mothers and fathers and, because she is a girl from Georgia, she always listens to her folks.

She stopped going to school in the seventh grade as she was the oldest child and had to watch the younger babies at home while her folks worked. Her parents could never tell who she was talking to because they had so many small ones around. They thought, "I was talkin' to one of them." Her father, she has told Joanne, turned her out onto the street when she was 18 years old.

"We was sittin' eatin' dinner one night and I was talkin' to someone next to him, but only Daddy couldn't see no one. He kept sayin' that the devil was in me and I had to go or else the devil would get all of them. There ain't no devil in me."

"I roamed around for a long time, sleepin' in those woods and freezin' at night. I ate rabbit and some berries. A voice told me to go to town and look for work, so I did, and that must've been the voice of God 'cause I got a good job livin' in and takin' care of a nice family's children. I cooked and cleaned a bit, and they gave me money and a room. I tried real hard to talk to the voices only when I was alone while I was livin' there.

"When this family moved north to New Jersey they took me with them. I knew that they felt sorry for me cause I had no family of my own. But that was okay, I really liked the kids and felt as though I wanted to still live with them. I was a little scared to move to the new place as I didn't know nothin' about New Jersey. But these folks was smart and real rich and they be sayin' they want me to go with them, and so I went. Either that or return to the woods again. The new house was a rough adjustment for these folks and the Mister and Misses started to fight a lot, and the kids grow'd up, and the time came too soon that they didn't need me no longer. They never told me so in those exact words, but I knows the way they was thinkin' 'cause I could see in their thoughts. One day I just took a train to New York City like the other folks did. I didn't want them to tell me I was not needed anymore like my folks did. Even with the voices tellin' me that I'd be alright, it was just too painful to hear that again.

"When I gots to the city it looked real angry. Nobody smilin' couldn't find a kid playin' ball in the yard nowhere, and for sure there were no damn rabbits nor berries. I took to sleepin' in the big places where people wait for trains and busses to come in. I wished that I had gone back to Georgia instead of this big place. I remember thinkin' this must be what it is like to die and go to hell.

"I must have been living in the Port Authority area for a few months before some people started to come around and talk to me and other people that were homeless. I never liked them comin' around askin' me questions about my life, and wantin' to know if I wanted to go to a hotel to live. My voice kept sayin' that I had no money for a hotel, so I kept sayin' no, I ain't goin'. These weren't my folks or my bosses, and I figured they couldn't tell me what to do. But there was a bad cold spell in 1983 and one of the women who slept on the bench in Grand Central Station froze to death one night. I decided then that when the people showed up again with their pads and pens and peanut butter sandwiches, I would go wherever they wanted me to."

She came to the shelter when it was run by the City of New York. They had many guards at the time, a metal detector, and served only cold food, three times a day. She said that she was always feeling hungry and tired. There were mice running all over the place. "They was constantly catching them in traps, and, at night, they could hear them going off. Now it is run by a private organization and it is much better. We have hardly any mice, and one guard."

The women in this shelter like to sit in the halls or in the basement and talk. A lot like to play Bingo, it keeps their hopes alive. They get angry when they don't win. Some get jealous. Theresa says that she has never had much, so she doesn't look for it. "I am happy watching the women folk live and die here, and to watch some have their dreams come true by gettin' their own apartments. For some of them it is the first time they ever had a place of their own. But, for me, I just want to stay here and listen to the voices in my own head and to see the world as it is in other people's heads," she says. Now, though, there are changes happening for Theresa as she may be moving as soon as the papers are processed through welfare. Joanne has also tried to get her to take medication to help the voices. She says when she hears them, she tells herself, "I'm not going to listen to you." She recognizes the voices to be the only bad part of herself that keeps her from being like the folks that walk to work in this neighborhood.

Sheena

"I'm gonna miss the women here and the workers, but the folks that live here will stay with me even after I am dead," says one client, Sheena, an elegant lady who dresses like she is going to business each and every day. The other clients have a lot of respect for her. But most of the women just want her to shut up. She rambles and talks sometimes all night long and no one can get any sleep.

Some of the women believe that she thinks she is special and things like that. Joanne, isn't sure if she even recognizes her or not. But it doesn't matter. She is committed to helping her. If Sheena can get dressed and is cognizant of the way the other clients see her, then she can be reached. Eventually. Hopefully.

Most of the women have beds in the large dorm where the sun, in the yellow strips of dust, drives through the old gymnasium window that now houses one-hundred-and-nineteen beds for ninety homeless women. To Sheena, who is in her seventies, it looks like Jesus himself is going to show up. She has said that she has seen Him and His classic, long reddish hair stringing around His shoulders, and that His gaze focuses on He who is higher than Him. Yes, the earthly image of the Son of God is coming: That's what Sheena says to the person next to her, who is invisible to everyone else. She points to each window, sixteen in all, forty-five feet from the floor. And then she rambles and rambles and staff try to snap her away from the delusion. She fades in and out of it, but she speaks to the aides and the maintenance crew, who get to hear most of it.

"He's in that corner over there," Sheena says, directing her index finger to the last window. "I told Him that my brother's wife did have a face lift, and that when we sat Shiva for him I could see the lines. There is no way that her

23

skin could stay that clear for fifty-six years. I pulled the hat off her head and told them all that she was always a liar and a cheat and that I could prove it. Look at the cuts behind her ears…you were there, Jesus, and when they grabbed me off her with her hat still in my hand, You told me that I was right, and she was a liar, and what kind of a Jew was I to use your name during my brother's Shiva? It was important that they know that if she lied about her face, she lied about his money and her other men. And she lived, and he didn't, and why did You take him from me? When is it going to be my turn?"

Sheena never leaves the gymnasium on time. Carlos comes in anyway and sweeps up wads of tissue drenched with human spit, then proceeds to wash the floors. Once these floors were highly polished with basketball lines in black and red. What is left other than the smell of urine and bleach is potential. Carlos has seen Sheena's nude body many times. He has heard her conversations with Jesus, her dead brother, a group of friends who show up in her locker mirror. He waits for the scent of bleach to get her dressed and out of the room. Sometimes Sheena hears the floor aide, Telley, in between the voices in her head.

"Let's go, Sheena, you're always the last one out. Carlos has to do his job. Don't you want the floors nice and clean?" Mostly, though, beyond Telley's manipulative words, which Sheena hears when she is in this reality, the smell would send her to the elevator, away from her locker. A one-by-eight-foot-long cabinet is where she hangs dresses and stashes *Lancome* cosmetics and two hair brushes that she has had since she was a kid in Germany.

Sheena spins her head toward the bright red emergency door, looks into its eyes and says: "You go to hell, you fucking bitch. Who are you to tell me? I know she was a liar. She cheated on my brother and he dropped dead of a heart attack trying to support her and her five fucking kids all Harvard grads and not one at Shiva." Sheena brushes her graying hair, works over the knot in her scarf, pats it flat against her chest, then looks at Carlos. "Ethel," she begins, "they put him in his grave prematurely…sixty-one years old. No chance to retire and see his grandchildren, to sit in the fucking Florida sun and burn up like a nice old Jewish man should. She got it all. The house. The business…" Carlos drops more bleach on the floor and waits. Sheena slams her locker and takes the elevator to the lobby and leaves the shelter for the next seven hours.

Wednesday, September 15, 1999

Frances watches a new homeless woman, who is twenty years younger than she, come into the shelter. She is a full-sized woman, about size 22, and her hair is long, black and white: It reminds Frances of crystal. She watches the new lady who wears a coat and sandals. Joanne hopes that Frances can start to talk now about her impending leaving. The past nine months have been a time of self discovery for her. She has never had therapy before. She has a special relationship with Theresa. And Joanne believes that Frances' leaving is agitating Theresa. Theresa's talking has been loud and angry. The shadows she owns and talks to are longer: The ones she lives with in alternate in dominance and permanence. Staring straight into Joanne's face, and not from her side view. The periphery communication, she has always been so good at, gives in and changes to a more direct contact with Joanne.

The new woman's bags are filled with make up and fancy perfume from a department store. Her name is Andrea. She is a Caucasian woman whom Theresa tries to understand. She looks fancy to Theresa, dressing up in front of a mirror that she has balanced on the dining room table in between two boxes. Andrea's dress is raggedy along the hem. She wears no stockings, but her hair and face are beautiful. She wears black and white eyeliner across the tops of her eyelids. Theresa is in the corner playing with the top button on her green sweater, her thin arms crossed over in front of her chest. She puts most of her weight and balance on her left leg, and then she continues to watch Andrea who shakes a small bottle rigorously until she stops, opens the cap, and puts the makeup on her face. The staff are starting to set the room up for lunch time. The aides fill the coffee pot with water and turn the spout to the inside wall so the women don't come over and try to take some while it is brewing. They get plates and cups out onto the serving tables for the meal. They check for the sugar.

Andrea continues to sit and to see only her own face.

# # #

Theresa stared at Frances as she grabbed her green sweater around her shoulders. It served her well, as she avoided physical communication with anyone and the very image of holding onto one's sweater gave the clear impression that she did not want anyone near her. But she was hearing the song again. Her favorite in her whole life, and so she grabbed the greenness between her fingers and intermittently patted her hair underneath the black scarf, while she remembered love from twenty-seven years ago.

Her eyes are clear and large. Her brows bold and black. Not bad for someone who doesn't go outside, who hides in a closet every chance she gets, and drinks black coffee all day long. Her feet are chalky looking in a white, scaly way. No socks. Just black pumps with a point in the front of the toe. She climbs up and down the staircase and sits in one of the shelter's dining room chairs at the bottom of the fourth floor landing in between the fourth and fifth floors. She pulls the sweater up and over her head when she needs to nap. No one bothers her. She inches her back along the walls when she hears loud voices from the women who scream for different reasons.

Theresa doesn't care much for screaming, heard plenty from home when she was growing up. But the others don't know, and scream out loud, forcing Theresa to take cover by either pushing her shoulders together or sucking on her fingers. Sometimes she does both things at one time: The shoulders go up and the fingers go right to her mouth. Her glazed eyes fix onto one object, her back against the wall until she gets to where she needs to be.

Today it's the dining room. She hasn't been eating enough lately, according to staff, but Joanne watches Theresa, without Theresa knowing, as she gets tea, cereal and a muffin. Theresa packs the food up, covering it with several napkins for the journey back to her seat in the staircase. The lights are dim and sparse in this area. The few other women who also sit in the staircase are readers and sleepers. Not generally an agitated group, but the few to watch for changes. It's those who don't draw much attention to themselves that the social workers need to be mindful of. Should changes in their dress, tone, speech, or habits arise there is probably something going on with them. Thus, the interest in Theresa who was already a slim woman, and when it was realized that she wasn't eating, they begin to take special notice of her. Frances walks in behind her. She's learning to be a social worker she says, "Hi Theresa, how's it going?"

"That song from the seventies 'Love Train,' it plays over and over in my mind now that I have heard it. Yesterday it was playing on the TV for a commercial and I was just makin' the cereal for myself and my old life in my family's house came a bouncin' backs to me. Like I was still livin' at home the song remindin' me of that boy who was always lookin in ma's window and specially whens I was cleanin' in the afternoon time. He be peekin' in at me like I couldn't see the top of his dark head. I pretendin' not to see him, as I was fancy on he, too. Daddy caught him one time and went a chasin' him with the gun. The boy was not too scared, thos', cause he kept a comin' back as often as he damn well pleased, and I liked it. And that song when I was a young'in filled up my insides with a lot of happy feelins that no one ever knows about. Not even today do they know that it is special to me. So then the song is playing on the TV for a commercial and I be so happy for the next few days that I be feelin' the good things inside of me like I was a young girl again. So's I be happy and feelin' less like eatin' and then the social worker comes tryin' to talk to me. I don't wants her here talkin' and tryin' to get me to say things. She be puttin' things into my mind that I don't want to be thinkin' about. All I want to do is remember the boy and she be tellin' me about livin' in a place of my own!"

Frances stands by Theresa without saying a word. She nods to let Frances know that she is listening.

Sixty-seven long, wide years of stomping her feet against the cement and watching as her dreams are dragged to their death. Theresa finds comfort in breezy walls that shed plaster like tears. There is no interest by the state to fix or repair the decay. Theresa likes it the way it is and prays for it to stay unchanged. She has seen shapes of her family carved into the walls. Fat-haired women proudly pumped out from curl and kink. Profiles of little girls with calf-length hemmed dresses and three-inch sashes around their small waists. Crinoline slips, too long, creeping out below the hem line, unbeknownst to the wearer. Her little brother's big head at five years old; she can hear his lisp.

"Thister," he calls, "come pull me in da wagon." Today he must be at least fifty years old, if he is still alive. He was a little *slow* to the rest of the world, but he was Theresa's favorite. He also wanted to play with the dolls and help her wipe the beds with the stick so the covers would be perfect, without lumps and uneven lines. He sat on her lap while she held conversations with invisible people. He put his head on her shoulder when she would sing songs. Theresa held onto her family in the lines of light that gleamed into the fortress. One-hundred-year-old, white plaster turns into the love she longs to have. With the sweater up over her head, she inhales her own carbon dioxide.

29

Theresa is mellow right now, the way she is most of the time, sitting in a borrowed, over-sized military chair. Her rosaries circle her hands. She wants to pray and to say one full Hail Mary for each bead, so she holds each one, heating it up with her body.

"Hail Mary," she begins, and her father shows up, "full of grace," he dallies as he puts on muddy shoes for work in the fields, "the Lord is with thee," he stands, pulls his suspenders up, and jollies his waistband with his thumbs.

Theresa's eyes widen in full scope. She looks at the walls, "and blessed is the fruit of thy womb, Jesus." On her mind is a vision to have the plaster remain unfixed and for her chair to stay where it is behind a railing of the staircase where there are no stairs. Just an over-look of a view of the ratty side of the building. The neglected one-hundred-and-twenty-five-year-old crumble in its vulnerability, paradoxically becomes the safest area for her to be. The smell of mildew washes over her. She thinks it's a good sign.

Theresa's head is tiny, and a perfect oval shape. Its curve is a moon against the rectangular spindles in the staircase. Shadows of lines behind each spindle tells the gentle social workers to be strict. They unwaiver when approaching the small figure who is darkened in the sparse light. So dark it is impossible to see her eyes. The jaw line so tight and defined lying atop her neck that is more like a full-grown flower stem.

She wears pants under her skirt, and stockings under her pants. Then a T-shirt under her blouse and the green sweater over the blouse. A hat goes over the scarf and a headband is under the scarf. Her feet stay bare inside her shoes, scoffing bacteria and viruses.

The exposed part of her lower leg has scars from cuts and infections. Pink indentations, some deep, like lunar craters. Theresa's too busy looking at her plaster family and talking to her unseen friends to worry about how dry her skin has become.

The door opens and the light that's thrown into the hallway is unfamiliar to Theresa: Pink toned in a creeping angle. It felt like Christmas when she was a kid in Alabama. The legs of a man stand in the way in the dark, she is unable to see who it is. Her name is called. She can't remember where she is. The smell is unmistakable, it's holly wafting in and pine cones dripping sap. Burned biscuits and the sound of corn heating up in oil, hitting the steel pot, smiles up her whole face. Silly-looking with her teeth out, Theresa in her childhood dimension, the man is her father, Jake. He doesn't like it when she stays in the room by herself. Too much to be done with all the little kids running around. Needing their noses wiped and their dinner made, who else was going to do it? She, the eldest of the family, had her calling determined by tradition and birth order. Finally, she leaves the hall assuming the legs in the silhouette to be the voice of her father. Once in the dining room she carries out her duties. Tonight, Theresa serves the clients and cleans up after they are done eating. She helps sweep the floor and wipes the crumbs into the palm of her hand.

The staff compliment Theresa for being so helpful this night. She even sits down and eats the spaghetti with meat sauce. Biting into a roll she reaches for the sweater, but it is not there. She jumps, looks around the room, and runs back down the hallway to the staircase, busts the door open and sees it on the chair. The military chair, with its soft leather, has managed to keep the indentation of her small body molded into it. It looks like she is still sitting there. Theresa's large eyes search the corners in the hallway. She covers her laughing mouth with her hands. The bones in her fingers ward off her smile. Her plastic bags are still around the chair. Flies nibble at the openings. Forty-watt

31

light bulbs keep the hall area dimly lit. The smell of aging fruit is heavy in the air, bordering on the rotting stage. *Larva season has arrived in the shelter.*

Consuelo

Consuelo was a large, light-skinned black woman who sat on the floor in the hall most days with all her belongings spread out, including her dolls. When she wasn't doing that, she was riding the elevator up and down to the basement, trudging up the stairs and down the street to the main avenue with her huge bags in tow. If you asked her where she was going she would say: "to Brooklyn."

Consuelo decorated herself with strands of aluminum foil snapped together to make a hat. She would also use cans and tie them onto her head to keep away the bad radiation, she would tell staff. You could be sitting in the hall and when you looked out, Consuelo would be doing her thing. Consuelo would sit in her psychotic mental state and seemingly unavailable she would say, "Watch where you are walking, you might fall and get hurt."

Consuelo, with her 300 pounds of glorious flesh, would strip down naked when it was time to wash herself. It would have been logical to get into the shower, close over the curtain, then wash that body down. But Consuelo took all her clothes off, in the hall, where everyone could see her and then proceeded to wash herself from a sink! The unsuspecting male staff would turn away real quickly when they caught sight of her. And who had time to prepare?

She was also an astounding piano player. Show tunes, standards, her songs would fill the large hall with her soft-soul music.

Consuelo carried with her three dolls. She would count the dolls, giving them each their own number, pointing with her finger, grinning all the while: "One, two, three." Then she would sit straight back in the chair giving her breasts full view of the world. Peeking out from rips in her blue dress, her full, dark brown nipples looked outward. "Pretty

33

baby," she would say, stroking number three's face. The doll smiles all the time for Consuelo. It is happy to be fed, to be sung to, and to hang out of Consuelo's large black pocketbook. The hair on the baby's head is straight and black. Her lips are red. They look like Consuelo, as they smile all the time. If you didn't know that she was carrying around large baby dolls and passed her by, trusting only your periphery vision to tell you what was there, you might think she was carrying around large loaves of bread. Brown-crusted rye or a well-done white: Unsliced.

Consuelo laughs and feeds her babies as they sit in the gray metal chairs. She sings to them while her breasts move side to side. One time, she tried to feed one from her breast. She joyfully pushed the baby into her chest, sang outward to the ceiling's fluorescent lights. From an opening in her dress she believed the baby was getting nourishment. It was hard to tell which number baby it was.

Consuelo likes to spread dry towels across the lunchroom tables and wash the babies on them. Her legs are large and defined with strong rows of fat. She can barely get her hand around her side to reach the middle of her back. She washes, powders their bodies and oils their backsides. She wraps them in baby blankets. She loves them.

"Pick up those friggin' dolls," Sally yells to Consuelo. At first Consuelo keeps the smile on her face so the babies can still see her that way. She continues to sing for a few seconds longer beyond Sally's anger. "God damn nut. Place is filled with fucking nuts. Singing to those little nigger babies. Stupid bitch."

Consuelo picks up a chair and holds it up like a bull is going to charge. She screams at the top of her lungs. She grabs two of her babies and shakes them. She picks up the last baby thinking she is Sally. "Get out of here," she yells. Then she throws the doll against the wall of cinder block and the head falls off. The baby's face still smiles and then Consuelo smiles too. She picks up the head and places it into a food cart on top of a pile of clothes. She grabs the other babies from the floor and takes her bags and sits in the hall. She holds the headless baby and sings, "The Days of Wine And Roses."

Consuelo left one time to get a physical examination after her social worker had tried many times to get her to agree to an examination for a lump on her arm. It turned out to be malignant and Consuelo never returned to the shelter again.

#   #   #

Lucielle is crying in the bathroom. She was in a meeting with her social worker in the back room where the meetings are held and while she was in there someone stole her coffee and blew their nose into her jacket. It was covered in mucus, still wet, and she just started to cry. She told Mandy that the staff start talking among themselves and tell all sorts of blame-the-lady stories and flavor all their quiet little offices with whispering, gossipy tones with nasty statements like: "Why did she leave the coat outside? She needs to be more responsible. She oughta know better than that, there are over 100 women living here and anything can happen."

#   #   #

Theresa is riding behind Joanne in the elevator. She speaks to her friend, the one in her mind, only. A new lady who roams the halls like she is still in a Sixth Avenue showroom and she acts as though she has a personal staff person taking care of her, gets on the elevator, too. She would be beautiful if it weren't for her profile. And then she turns around and you see the most beautiful face. The face of an angel. Everyone gets lost in the beauty of her long black hair, not really straight, and her turquoise eyes. She presents like she comes from money. Always running away and around in circles like a puppy when it's new and running around on the floor outside its box.

She went to get clothes from the donation area. Her clothes were ragged, and her feet filthy from walking and dancing barefoot on Park Avenue. She kept chatting about her mother and how her mother was going to send some money soon when her credit got good again. A big grown-up woman who was still waiting for her mama. A big spoiled princess. But she was up in the special area where they give out clothes and she kept getting up and down up and down saying what she liked. The staff kept telling her to sit down and to stop jumping up and down that she wasn't allowed to go through the clothes, it wasn't a store. She was in a shelter and it's run a certain way. She can't just come up here and grabbing onto anything that she wanted. She was without shoes and she kept asking for a pair in size seven.

"You must have something for me," she kept saying like she was on the Riviera. She wanted the staff to please her and take care of her. She wanted to be waited on and have the clothes brought to her like she was a rich and famous person. She lives at the shelter for one whole week and she arrives and leaves wearing the same clothes and no shoes on her feet. She was walking up town in the neighborhood on the weekend and someone spotted her with no shoes on then either. She was wearing the same stockings and the same raggedy pants and shirt. But she wanted fine clothes. Not just shelter stock.

She told anyone who will listen that they need to eat vegetables only. That's what women need to feed themselves and anything else is "very, very bad for zee zystem." Her accent like a rich lady. Not like the rich folks in New York, but the European kind that no one can touch. Her accent is thick with French culture. And she speaks to all, to no one and she says, "Zere are sze flower shops szhat have such the beautiful smell of sze flowers and the powder of sze flowers, but there is no flowersz. There is sze vunderful psyzcik there too and she is jus so good, my friend and I will be going again szoon. He is coming again szoon and vwe vwill see sze vwunderful stores."

Theresa is aware of a lot about her roommates. She doesn't know about the rich lady's son, Matthew, who calls the shelter looking for his mama. His un-medicated, paranoid schizophrenic mother who can only tell him to be a good boy and to eat all of the vegetables that his grandma gives to him. The boy calls three times today asking if his mother is there yet. He, at eleven years old, adopted the doom of premature parenthood. Now he is the father of the mother. Today, he becomes a man. Not when he is Bar Mitzvahed, not when he has his first love affair, but from here on in, as he takes care of his mother. Homework and friends are now secondary to the child: He learns from now on how to hide a large piece of his life behind video games. He prays for her to return to him. To be like other mothers, maybe a little too fat, maybe a little too dull. Her sparkle, creativity, and esoteric inclinations, as she hovers between realities, is horrifying to him. Matthew is smart, but he feels bad inside when he thinks of his mother in a shelter. He envisions a tomb that is underground. That it is dark and there are many spiders crawling under the beds and up the walls. He is afraid that she is scared. He wants to protect her. Matthew takes the pictures of his mother with him when he was a baby and keeps them on his dresser next to his bed. He wants to remember her the way she was in the pictures, but he cannot.

Karen Maxwell

ATTACHMENTS

Karen Maxwell

Thursday, September 16, 1999

Open the packets and pour sugar down into opened,
junkie mouths, the sweet substitute disappears by the
hundreds. The staff cannot keep the sugar out in between
meals, at fourteen dollars per box, that could last one day; it
is too costly to keep putting a out a new box. It depends on
how many mica (mentally ill chemically abusing) women
they have living at the shelter. Junkies eat sugar like they
drink water. Open the small packets, six at a time, then
drop the sweet, grainy substance down the backs of their
throats.

Sometimes, all the women look the same, as though
they came from the same family. Hundreds of thousands of
years ago a stare that the parent had, still with them today, a
stare of catatonic poise. Looking off into the distant layers
of family and history, personal and newly experienced,
when the disease starts to take over a life, one by one, they
inevitably have the same look. Depressed people, paranoid
schizophrenic's, manics with their highs, as when someone
like Mary grabs the industrial-size mop and starts to clean
the massive floors. And then the lows the feelings of
worthlessness so deep and dark that one can't get the energy
together to flush the toilet, brush her teeth, or to eat.

Sweet Frieda from Chad, Africa, who snaps into a rage
when her chair is bumped accidentally by another, or Mrs.
O'Brien from Ireland who smiles and passes out flowers to
open hands, then throws the phone across the room when
she is feeling challenged. Perhaps through the cellular
history of homeless women, we can suspect that they know
one another. Origins of creation documented in the same
looks or glares or responses, one family gathered together in
the shelter spirit under a 20th-century roof.

The shelter, in its design during the development stage of paper work to program, is supposed to be a stop off before the women are placed into a more permanent housing situation.

On the way out of the building, one of the women who stayed too long in the mother shelter is Ms. Beatty, as she likes to be called. Now, Ms. Beatty is slipping off a chair in the basement.

She's got her own right to be here. Watch how she dresses in cow girl boots and plaid hats. Check out the brown skin that is shined up like a Cadillac from all that grease on her sixty-eight-year-old face. The damn navy blue raincoat, so ingrained with homeless lady all over it, its secret given away by the smell and style. Old donor-looking piece of garment, New York City folk too sophisticated not to tell that it was given to her. Not matched with the boots, the hair, the cap. She carries too many bags just to be shopping and she, like the other ladies, knows that the world sees her as different from the rest.

Now we are looking at Ms. Beatty who was kindly asked yesterday to leave the shelter when it was discovered that she stole someone's wallet with a whole lot of money in it: Couple of hundred dollars, at least three big ones, that would have put the lady who lost the money out of commission for most of the month.

They sent Ms. Beatty to a hotel to stay, like the shelter, and she went with the same clothes on. Some saw the plaid hat fall onto the floor when the cops put her into the elevator, and she was crying, too. She was accustomed to roaming the streets back and forth when she was one of the sheltered ladies at this shelter. Brave with all the patterns that she would wear in her clothes, fabrics speaking out for her what she couldn't say for herself. Ms. Beatty would strangle herself with pocketbooks and kept one raggedy pocketbook inside the other with tissues crumpled and chewed on. Natty pieces of ripped paper and a small detective novel always underneath her arm, keeping her shoulder still and her turn-around rigid. Over and over, Ms. Beatty promised that she was going back to Michigan, that she had real family there that wanted her in the mid-western state.

For the past six hours she has been sleeping on the chair in the basement where she doesn't belong anymore. Her hat is tilted and, the visor casts a shadow across her face. Her eyes aren't visible to those who look in her direction, but she can see who you are. And that's how she wants it. Ms. Beatty waits on the chair, not believing that the mother shelter doesn't want her any longer. Wait she does in the basement, drunk and exhausted. She walked two miles from the hotel with all her bags just to sit on the plastic chair, fall off it, and told to go back.

"Now, that ain't right," she says. "I ain't done nothing wrong and I ain't never stole nothin' in my whole life." She wants the director father to tell her that it's okay and she can come back upstairs now. That it was all a big, terrible mistake and that they know she never did, never would, steal someone else's wallet. "I won't do it no more," she mutters. Ms. Beatty slides off the chair while holding most of her bags. Many more bags are on the floor around her. It looks like she has been shopping instead of her having all her possessions in the world around her. She smells of fried chicken and spicy Greek potatoes. Her navy blue socks are sinking into her white, high-heeled sneakers. Most feel sorry for Ms. Beatty, but the sorrow is short lived when they remember what she has done to the other old lady.

Frances comforts the old lady who was ripped off. She has become more fearful than before. There is talk among the managers about the fearfulness that is spreading among the women. If Theresa wasn't leaving soon, Joanne would talk to her about her focus and where it needs to be. On her, not on others. But Joanne lets it be. Perhaps the fact that she is helping others is helping her to become stronger. But she can't be sure.

The shelter is a twenty-four, hour facility, seven days a week. It has three shifts of aides and managers each day. There is a pre-formed way that staff are trained to behave toward the women. Listen to them, don't let them in on your life, keep your personal issues to yourself. Be fair. Be consistent. The challenge to this is that when the women let staff in on their lives they begin to identify with them. They are alike, after all. They come from unhealthy family backgrounds, but nevertheless still had families. A beginning. A childhood. One woman who went to see a Broadway show for the first time and was in her sixties, said: "Imagine me going to a Broadway show."

# # #

Reception desk. Stationed on the third floor, the nucleus of the shelter, the core; the tit where they come to talk, ask questions, the same ones over and over again. Do I have mail? Check box number 48, check box number 67, is my social worker in today? Where are the diapers? Can I get soap? Toothpaste? Is Ms. Linda giving us a birthday party this month? Phone calls come in for the misplaced of the displaced of the disenchanted; the lost mothers and aunts and sisters of society. The wombs of earth emptied and void of any material usefulness. Abandoned by their own creation of themselves. Colors, sizes, smells, sucking the juice from the politicians who envisioned human needs on yellow-lined paper. Proposals, budgets, broken pencil tips, and directors who were hoping to fly the mother-shelter ship beyond the seat of their pants, forgetting that what was on their side was spirit.

Celeste

Celeste is getting ready for Thanksgiving even though it is September. She asks Joanne, "Do you know where I was this time last year?" Joanne has no idea, really, and tells her so. Celeste looks healthy, with a normal spread of post menopausal flesh across the mid section of her body. A slight trampling of extra chin on her face that she doesn't notice when she looks into the mirror. Celeste is Hispanic, yet never speaks in Spanish. She listens, shakes her head, and answers in English.

Flashes of different living situations go through Joanne's mind. Was Celeste in another shelter? Perhaps the Brooklyn Women's Shelter? A house of her own? Joanne is not Celeste's social worker, and she wonders why she is telling her this?

"I was riding on the A train," Celeste says, interrupting the pictures Joanne is having of her in her head. She then stopped dreaming and focused on Celeste's face. Her skin soft in between the wrinkles, the kind that makes a woman look like she is in her sixties. She thinks about her grandmother and the corsages she wears on holidays. Celeste wanted to talk and Joanne accepted her engagement.

"How did you end up on a train?" Joanne asked.

"My boyfriend beat me. I left the house to get a quart of milk for his dinner and never went back. I wanted to be free."

"What was it like living on the train?"

"After three weeks some teenagers cut me up and robbed me. They took everything I had. I ended up in a hospital where I stayed for a few days. I never knew what a social worker was before this happened to me."

Celeste is happy and it seems almost inappropriate to Joanne that she could be so nonchalant about her abuse.

45

She wears a red shirt that clashes with her olive-toned skin. Her straight black hair is pulled off her face with a white headband. Celeste searches Joanne's eyes, from the top of the black in her pupil to the bottom, she watches without blinking. She dissects Joanne's response to her by watching her muscles. When her pupil recedes in the light, she waits for it to dilate.

Joanne continues to have visions of Celeste on the train, sleeping, eating, using the train station bathrooms, using the bathrooms in department stores. Dragging around her bags that are getting dirtier by the street. Dreaming in public. Reading on the train. She assume her diagnosis to be manic depression with schizophrenia. How many must have walked past her on their way to work or school or doctors' appointments. Stench from her body keeping them away. Her teeth, unblemished, white and wide: Of a woman who never bore children. She looks like a milk drinker, but she loves beer and cheap wine.

Celeste has lonely eyes that she can't help but show. They weep in form after sixty years of unloving lovers and a large family that loved the little Celeste from their stupor. Circles of alcoholics from one roof top to another. The addresses changed, but the party went on year after year for Celeste until she was smack on the A train in 1999 as it cruised Ph.D's, and MBAs to hundred-thousand-dollar-a-year jobs and AA classes.

She could have been as lucky to have had one person somewhere at some point in her six-decade journey believe in her. But Celeste has no regrets. "I'm so happy to be here today. It's so warm, and everyone is so nice to me. Mr. Lopez is helping me to get my own home, I can hardly believe it. The director says that there are dishes I can have, and he thinks there is a television that someone donated. I told Mr. Lopez that please, all I would like to have the most of anything is a view of a bridge. I don't care if it's

Williamsburg, or that New Jersey bridge. I just love to look at the bridge at night. It helps me to believe my dreams to come true. And if I can look then at a bridge each night, then there will be no more for me that I need."

Chynna Maryanne

For some, even though it is springtime, people are in the winter of their lives. Not only do the women in the shelter live complicated lives, but the staff are busting with challenges as well.

The shelter would not function if it were not for the program aides and the maintenance staff. They do most of the dirty work.

Time had come for Chynna Maryanne to move out of the shelter. They had tried to place her in outside housing twice before and the final time was when they found a supervised community residence in Brooklyn. They had prepared her for the interview, and she went for the visit and they submitted her paperwork and she was accepted. But she was having the dreams more and more. They were coming into the forefront of her consciousness about the babies.

Chynna Maryanne dresses in pale blue all the time. In windy fabrics that move like tissue in winter; after showers, while she is still wet, she dresses herself in light powder blue. The color clings to her dark skin and reflects off her tiny Spanish face, softening the years. She talks about her baby girl, the one who went to live with her mother while she was living in Cuba. Chynna Maryanne wants soap and towels and she talks about the soul of her baby back on the isle bonita Cuba. "My baby is beautiful and my mommie has her, so soon I go home and spend time with my baby."

Chynna Maryanne says she has dreams of flying babies. That she reaches out in the dark, crowded dorm when the babies start to come. Sometimes, as many as twelve babies float by her, suspending themselves, barely, and then they seem to drop slowly like helium balloons. She reaches for one, hoping that she can grab onto an ankle or a hand, but then they disappear.

Her beautiful baby is now seven years old, but Chynna Maryanne has not seen her for that long and therefore cannot imagine her any way other than as a baby. "It was on a boat that I escaped and it was unbelievable because it was raining and the waves were very high. I believed that my baby would come with her father, but her father was killed and so now my life is with no one. It is not the way I planned it to be. I hope that soon I can see my girl."

Chynna Maryanne tells the story the way she wants it to be known, but there is another reality. She won the lottery that Cuba has for its citizens to leave the country, and she decided to take it. She made a choice to get out of Cuba and to leave her daughter behind. The baby's father abandoned both of them years ago when he left on a boat to the United States. Today she is asking for more toothpaste and a new toothbrush. She wears them out because she brushes her teeth all the time. She covers her wet hair in a blue scarf to match the dresses in the same color. Her dark skin glows with pink. She hardly looks old enough to have a baby and yet she is forty-six years old. She shines with virginity. Coquetishly, she talks with the maintenance men who understand her Spanish. They are sympathetic toward her, but behind her back they think that she was wrong to have left her baby behind. What kind of life could be lived without the child that she bore, they wonder aloud when she is not around to hear them. She tries to get their sympathy and kindness, this helps her to feel better about what she has done. In the daytime, when she can no longer depend on the dreams that make it possible for her to hold her girl, she cleans and scrubs away little reminders that are on her skin. The pain distracts her from her thoughts for awhile.

The social workers want Chynna Maryanne to visit alternative housing and to start to plan on moving out. She has been living in this shelter for five years. She has tremendous fear that if she leaves her family will never be able to find her. So she slips away when her social worker is looking for her and hides in corners of the great armory. She eats her meals in the staircases, sometimes sharing them with Theresa Mills. They struggle to understand each other's language, yet understand each other perfectly well. In pointed moments of protection, they hide the knowledge of each other's whereabouts. Standing alone for years and years, fighting off the unknown, they collude like astral comets every now and again and stand up for each other.

Chynna Maryanne looks forward to the night time when the shelter gets dark and she can lie down and be silent again. Quieting the escape she took, one day years ago, to leave her poverty-ridden country. Hushing the sunshine of the daylight and the visions and voices of young children playing on swings and jumping on ropes. In the dark, she lies down and waits for the sweet babies to come floating by her once again.

The social workers tell her that she can dream in her new home. That the babies will follow her there.

The guilt she has felt for abandoning her daughter has day by day claimed Chynna Maryanne's life. Frozen in the experience of the lost heart, her psychosis and delusions feed her. They make it okay for her to be where she is.

"If I leave the shelter then what would my baby do when she comes to look for me and I am not here? You don't understand, I cannot leave the shelter, ever."

Friday, September 17, 1999

It's three thirty in the afternoon and Frances is sitting on her bed, sorting through her belongings. She lifts up her mattress and takes out four novels. She holds one in the air. "Does anyone want this?" she asks. Most of the women are lying down on their beds. A few of the women have jobs during the day so their beds are empty. Vivian clops over to Frances in her broken shoes and takes the book without knowing that it is the Holy Bible. Frances smiles. Joanne waves to her from the doorway when she sees her. With her back now turned, her silhouette replaces her face. She is now a client, a body mass taking up a bed in a shelter. In a few days she will take back what she struggled for so long to keep: her dignity, her life, her own place to live.

Theresa follows Joanne while she watches Frances. She swallows Joanne up in a face-to-face view this time. She speaks to Joanne face forward. Joanne holds onto her steps. She tries not to blink. Then Theresa speaks: "Frances is really leavin'?"

Joanne pauses almost too long before she answers. "Soon, she's leaving in a few days."

"They thinks that I crazier than I is. Today I was found hidin' in a closet but I wasn't hidin' like they would hide. I was in there to get away from all the noise in here. Always so much noise, and I can'ts hear the voices. A visitor was in the building looking at the shelter and she saw this closet and then opened it. The director got a bit mad at me and tole me that I shouldn't go in there. I knows that he saw me in there many times before and I thinks that he only say that so's he could look smart. Treatin' me like I was a kid and had to be tole what to do. I knows much better but there is not one corner that I can find to be mine. This is whys I lives in the staircase where it be quiet and at night I listens to the wind blow.

51

"But there's a woman who be remindin' me of my daddy and I gets scared when she comes by me. The voices in my head keep me company. I have two voices today and we talk back and forth. And even one be tellin' me to go to the closet, not to let them see me cause they be tryin' to poison me today. So's I starts thinkin' about the poison and what kind they would have like for rats the kind that daddy was usin' for the rats that could stand taller than the youngin' in the family. He be beatin' them all the time in the cotton bags. I don't eats the lunch after hearing this, but my stomach be hurtin' so bad that I had tea instead. I be watchin' the man fill the tea pot and watchin' sos' no one could put nothin' in it then waitin' for it to get hot and I tooks' a tea bag from the bottom of the bin they has to hold it next to where the sugars is kept too.

"There are soldiers that walk in here from the 1892 year. Theys quiet and smokes a lot of rolled cigarettes. I tries to stay away from them when they be smokin' but in the June month it gets especially hot in here. They be askin me why I be hidin' my face when I laugh and that's I don't need to. My little sisters was always laughin' at me when I be laughin' without coverin up my mouth. Sos' I learnt to do this and now I don't want to shows my mouth to no one.

"I sees the soldiers drinkin' the coffee and ridin' on horses back and forth to the uptown farm and down to the farms. Central Park they is sayin' is where the shanties' is and the poor peoples be livin'. They be talkin' about the sheep in the park and that the houses in the park are goin' to come down soon. They don't know where the folks that are livin' in them are goin' to go, they's just know that the governor wants the park now for folks to have for flowers and for walkin' in.

"Then the soldiers leave away and this big lady sees me and asks the soldiers too if they can stop the radiation that is comin' into the shelter. She says, 'not the sun! I'm talkin' about the holes in the ceiling that they be makin' in here so the women get sick and die.'

"Theresa," Joanne begins, afraid of offering any insight or help as Theresa runs away clutching herself to herself. Then Joanne can't seem to find Theresa's body, or her mind, irregardless of how hard she tries to. But thankful for the interruption from Theresa, giving her more of who she is in an unstructured moment in the hallway.

#   #   #

Lunch arrived late today. Expected time of arrival? 11:00 AM. Delivery typically comes around 10:45 AM and the women start to line up about 11:45 AM while the aides set up the food, getting it ready for servicing. The line of women zig zags along the wall, their bodies leading out into the hall.

Mandy gives Joanne half a smile. She leads her life with little complication, which for some may be complicated. She shifts back and forth, from one foot to another.

Sigrid comes off the line when she sees Joanne and asks her for money for cigarettes. "I gave you money for cigarettes yesterday," Joanne says. "That's the agreement we had: Tuesdays and Fridays. If you drink alcohol then there is no money for two weeks. Do you remember this discussion we had?"

Sigrid wanders away from Joanne, her gray hair stringy from too much grease.

The lunch finally arrived and Joanne followed the delivery guy into the dining room. Thomasina was inching her way to the garbage cans. Staff caught her eating from them last week. She tells staff not to feel sorry for her or to approach her, that there is nothing wrong with her. She tries to tell them that she is looking for tin hearts with chocolate in them.

Joanne stops her: "Thomasina, not the garbage cans. Not today!"

The delivery man is taking the food containers off his hand truck. "Clinton's in town," he says, "the UN." Joanne let it go at blaming Bill.

Kathy

Joanne spots Kathy coming in to the dining room, looking at the food. Her elegant Kathy who backs up when anyone gets too close to her. Walks away in the opposite direction when someone walks toward her.

Kathy, so good at stepping over large bags. She was coming into the dining room for a cup of coffee. Kathy kept her head covered with a white scarf and more often than not a separate scarf to cover her mouth. Not that it was improper to show one's face, as if she was a Moslem; Kathy was afraid that someone would recognize her.

Joanne was able to learn some of Kathy's history from her which was that she came from a large city, had two daughters over 30 years ago, and was married once. Kathy also revealed that she had had a lover during her marriage, and that he had brought her so much bliss, and so much pain, that when he'd left her she simply stopped living. Shortly after coming to the shelter, eleven years ago, she'd decided to remain in the shelter forever, where she could have freedom to do what she wanted and to also be unknown.

During one session she did take off the scarves and talked. The most important thing in her life, the one thing she lived for, was this man. She called him Jim and she met him in the early 1970s at the beach, while her little daughters played in the sand.

"He was just there," she said, "with the most magnificent color skin I had ever seen. Tan skin, almost dark brown, but he was Spanish, so it just looked tan to me. His hair was black and straight like an Indian's. But it was the way he was lying on his blanket, trying to fix his radio, that began our conversation." He was kind to her, when her husband wasn't. He didn't enjoy getting drunk like her

55

husband did, nor did he take her for granted. Whenever they met, they danced, and he held her tightly around the waist until she melted into him. "He told me that I was beautiful, and damn if I didn't feel it every time he said it to me." Jim gave Kathy more love than she had ever had in her whole life and she just couldn't give it up.

"Jim was patient and he listened to me when I talked about how I wanted to be an actress. He told me I could do it, that I could be whatever I wanted to in life because I was very talented, and I could do a great imitation of Betty Davis. He would laugh and laugh, and then I would laugh with him."

Kathy admitted to loving her girls. She said that she never meant to hurt them. "Sometimes when you have children, you think they will be small forever. Day in and day out, everything goes to them. Even when you're not with them, they are with you. Your next move is for what they need, and sometimes you think: Will it ever end? That this is it! Forever and ever you will have to do everything all day long just for your kids. Wash their clothes, shop for groceries, clean the house, throw out garbage, and deal with schools and their friends and then their boyfriends, pay bills, deal with their father, for their sake. Then this stranger on a blanket with tan skin sees me differently and I fall in love with him."

"What kind of work did he do?" Joanne asked.

"He was an artist. He painted abstract art on large canvases and he traveled all over the world with his art for exhibitions. I wanted to go with him. I wanted to see the world as he did. He painted my body in a portrait and someone bought it. I was nude, but that didn't bother me until my husband found out. My husband beat me until my body and face looked nothing like the painting, so no one could recognize that it was me, he said. When I got out of the hospital everything was gone. No husband, no kids, no

Jim. No home. I walked the streets some nights, and for awhile I took a job as a clerk in an automotive outlet store. Sometimes it was hard to get out of bed when I was thinking of Jim. I haven't seen my girls since they were 16 and 18 years old. No one knows where I am and I don't want them to know."

Kathy took her white scarf and wrapped it around her face. She took the second one and wrapped it around her head. It was the last time she talked to Joanne that way. After that, she tried and tried to get Kathy to talk more about Jim and her daughters, but the cover-up stayed, and Kathy would only listen from there on in.

Kathy's heart was stuck at the sandy beach and in the nude portrait that Jim had painted of her. She didn't know that in life there is the *self*, the *herself* that she needed to get close to before others came to her. She dreamt about Jim during the days and the nights. That love from twenty years ago would become the premise of comfort for Kathy for the rest of her life.

Her delusions bloomed like an ugly flower. Her lust for anonymity replaced her sexual passion.

The dining room fills up today. Rita and Sigrid sit next to each other until Sigrid realizes that Rita smells of urine and then decides to move. Stanley, a big guy with a gentle voice comes in to get lunch.

"Whatcha' havin'?" the aide asks.

"Some of everything."

"Stop fleecing the lunch," Mrs. O'Malley yells out. Stanley ignores her and takes his food to the staff lounge. But, no matter what the shelter feeds the women, how they clean their linens, what exercises they provide for them to better their outlook, the women go on in their own ways.

Donita

They live. They continue to beat on in spite of smoking three packs of cigarettes each day, high blood pressure, and cholesterol readings in the three hundreds, they live. Sleeping in rows with three-foot-wide aisles keeping in code with the Department of Homeless Services, and one-hundred-and-nineteen women in the dorm on mattresses large enough for a big kid, they live.

Curled into the womb effect, the chair almost large enough to hold Donita's one-hundred-and-thirty pounds of 48-year-old-living. Hairy spots in her head, now brittle with grayness, not the way she says the world is towards her. Distant and blaming it is to her, she says. Always against her, and not the others. Why me? She argues with bags and bags of plastic containers that she cleans many times a day. Red hands cracked and sore from her obsessive-compulsive disorder; each day staff hope that she moves out of the shelter. But where would she go? A tough one to deal with, Donita, who looks cute all the time, but whom staff just want to run away from when she asks if she can talk to them for a minute. Only one manager has dealt with her effectively by giving her the *no* on most things. *No,* then walk. The way she checks the bags around her bed twenty, thirty, forty times before she leaves the dorm, is the way she also is with people. Back and forth checking her opponents, mind, examining the words and using them against the other when she wants her way. Accustomed, no doubt, to having this tactic work in the past, frustrated with this shelter, as now her old ways aren't accepted. Donita wants to manipulate and talk others into her views to have the managers and aides give her what she wants and not question or doubt her and she can't have it.

Donita walks into the shower every day and doesn't come out to wash her hands and wipe her hair with a towel for six hours. The shower stall is layered with white plastic bags that she washes before and after she leaves. All six clothes hooks hang with her immaculately clean plastics. The water runs and runs before she steps into the stall to remove debris from the pipes and the possibility of rust getting on her. The thought harasses Donita's mind. Dirt is her executioner. Tiny particles of bacteria will torture her imagination for hours and days. Any one of them could get her at any time. Then suddenly she falls asleep on the chair, snarled into the seat, like a hairless cat.

Donita has held jobs, and was the daughter of a doctor in Scarsdale. Her diction reflects education; the way she carries herself is poised. Donita is never wrong. Her rights are impinged on if she is asked to leave the bathroom when it has to be cleaned.

The skin on Donita's face is sensitive to air and light; she covers every part of her body before she leaves to go outside. The other women tend to think that she has special treatment. That she is permitted to shower for most of the day, walk around barely dressed, and get extra baby lotion for her delicate skin, is disconcerting to them.

Donita has been passed around for most of her adult life from one relationship to another. She has a degree in Hospital Administration and she tells the staff all the time that they don't know what they are doing.

When no one is there to speak for the mentally ill, they perish.

Peggy

The *Daily Word* lies unopened next to Peggy's coffee cup. Her head is thrown so far down while she sleeps in the chair that she looks like a shelf. She is adorned with a 1960s solid silver barrette, blackened where the silversmith gently engraved the scene of a horse entering its barn. A large bobby pin holds back more hair just behind it. Wearing black patent leather boots with set-back heels, shoulder length gray hair recently cut, she looks up from the heat of Joanne's analysis and smiles. Her dentures are too large, the lipstick—kissable red—shaped into a bow; nice contrast in form against the rectangular barrette and her oval face. There is no history on Peggy. Somebody loved her, since she knows how to act lovingly.

Then what happened, in a simple assessment, is that she got hurt. Someone placed her heart in the way of a closing door and slammed it. She never saw it coming. After that she stayed in one spot thirty years too long, wearing away the ground. Not noticing when people around her left or died, she continued to stay on her spot until the city found out that there was a crazy lady whose apartment door couldn't be opened because of the garbage inside. Still, she wasn't fazed. She begged for money, slept all the time, and fixed herself up in front of the mirror in dirty, wrinkled, dead clothes when she had to go out and beg.

Her mood is 1960s glamour, or Hollywood does hippieville. Occasional golden threads are in her sweaters, long sleeved and v-necked. She is sweet, and stuck in the moments before the door slammed. Peggy, with clear eyes and a child's spirit, whom the other clients run to help and protect and feed. The shelter society's baby naps on and off and they cover her with a blanket, offer her tea, and coax the darling to take her medicine.

On this day some old friends came to see Peggy, she was prodded to get up from the chair that she claimed to be hers, dragging it from room to room.

"Who?" she asked, her bow lipstick seeping into the fine lines around her mouth.

"You've got some visitors today, some folks are here to see you," another resident said.

Peggy looked out toward the reception desk where three eager older women waited. Shopping bags were on the floor around their feet. They hadn't unbuttoned their coats, nor taken off their hats. They smiled in earnest. "Never saw them before in my life," Peggy said smiling the way she does with the big dentures. Then she looked again, stood up, turned her seat completely around to face the wall.

The three women visitors were asked to leave their bags at the desk for their friend. Peggy's long, gray hair doesn't get any brighter under the light that she is now beneath. She keeps her eyes open as if she is hearing with them, until she hears the elevator door open and the visitors leave.

The bags are brought over to her so she can open them up. She smiles the whole time, letting others look into the bags, taking out a new pair of boots, cookies, and three wrapped gifts each with different wrapping. She takes the red ribbon and tries to wrap it into her hair. It falls to the floor. Red like her face, like she was trying to kiss herself.

The women lurched along the halls today. Frances was avoiding eye contact with Joanne as she entered the countdown to her leaving the shelter for her own place to live. The shelter pushes independent living onto dependent women. They counsel and support their personalities and weed through their mental illnesses. Side by side, the women sift through the air, some like leaves on trees. Today, Frances is a transparent oak.

61

Her silence was a different way of communicating. Her wrangling away from final words with Joanne was screaming out that a different Frances was emerging. Was this the way she learned to say good-bye in her life? By avoiding feelings? If she doesn't speak about them then they don't exist?

Dejavu ricocheted around Joanne like a jigsaw puzzle. Rickrack cut edges couldn't fit together. The pattern had a life of its own, separate from Joanne, it was Frances and the relationship they had. Joanne knew she had to keep at Frances, and she would do so right until the last 45-gallon plastic garbage bag filled with her possessions was put into the taxi for her. Even after Joanne gets to close the car door, she will watch until it turns the corner to let Frances know that the lines would still be open between them.

Mary, another social worker on the team, notices the shift in dynamics that have begun between Frances and Joanne. Does Joanne want her to talk to Frances? she wants to know.

"About what?" Joanne says. "Frances and I have to see this through, as you have done with Betina who has become harder and harder to reach." Mary dutifully checks in with Betina who sometimes hears her social worker, and so they rumble through the jumble with, slow walkers, and tired asses, signing away their dignity in exchange for a bed, sociologically effective groups, and prying social workers who turn into Lucifer upon approach.

"Don't come near me you son of a bitch. Who told you to talk to me?" Frequently expressed phrases like this screw into the ears of those who listen.

Betti

Betti sits in her pissed in clothes on the plastic chair, saying "hello mon," Jamaican accent winding around her high cheekbones. Clutching a black handbag, she sat one day next to a garbage can that was smoking from a dropped cigarette. Betti, unable to see or process the danger she was in, remained stone-eyed, nicotine fixed, and dementia-ridden. Her purple, sheer, polyester party dress draped like a perfect "U" between her legs. Betti wears white socks and black sneakers. She always manages to have her hair straightened, page-boy styled, black and shiny to the follicle. She is ready for a party, and waiting for it to happen. Betti carries an ID card so that if she wanders away and is found, she is returned to the shelter. Betti ebbs in and out of reality; sometimes she is very much a part of the earth plane. Other times she wanders and gets lost in the green horizon and the beaches of Jamaica. Attached to the shelter like a fetus lodged on the outside of the womb, unable to get back inside, or to get it right, because she is undocumented. Immigration Naturalization Service says Betti, and her like, are illegal people. "Got no papers, get no benefits." The shelter staff clutch the old lady to their breasts like Tarzans and Janes, swinging full force at the monkeys in government.

Flies hover around her bed as soon as the weather gets warm. Betti's hidden fruits revealed by nature's most profound sleuth: The timing of carcass-eating vermin, taking turns from their almost undetectable larvae stage, until they become a funnel of flies. "No mon, got no food in my bed mon," she says.

Lynn

Another bed wetter, is an established alcoholic named Lynn. Lynn doesn't drink, nor does she wet her bed, she says. The smelly room is the worst in the shelter, and it is where Lynn sleeps. Adult, female urine prompted by booze-filled bladders is the worst of the smells. It goes through your whole face jarring the sinuses into repair like a good sniff of ammonia. The worst part is that one is never prepared for the hit. There is no forewarning.

Lynn grew up in this Upper East Side of New York City and is so ill with alcoholism that she wanders the neighborhood at fifty-eight-years old, believing that she is still a schoolgirl on her lunch break. She wobbles on her cane in and out of Madison Avenue shops with too-pale make-up on her purple-and-blue-splotched face. Capillaries in her skin rising to the surface, due to years of strain from alcohol. Last July she spent night after night sleeping in the local park with her big Pioneer Supermarket shopping cart. Smoking and pushing the thing from bench to bench, pissing on herself, and hiding cheap bottles of alcohol. Living off liquid shit. Whatever food she eats is of little value to her nutritionally. So much poison taking the place in her stomach and liver of much-needed doses of potassium. Her fingernails are chipped and blackened underneath, competing with turning the stomachs of those who also smell her. Then she's got on red lipstick and brown eyebrows, feeling good for a few moments when she puts it on. Believing when she looks at you that you see her as she wants you to see her, not as she is: a rotting, living corpse, wasted and crawling around, the shelter becoming an alcoholic with her. The staff are drunk with their own beliefs that they are powerful and powerless. A constant contradiction explained away in treatment and psychotherapy and by psychiatrists who know, but fail to admit, that they are intoxicated, too, on the diseases of humans. Sometimes burrowing themselves like the occasional lice outbreak into the lives of the living dead: *One-hundred-and-nineteen women on any given night, one hundred different_stories.* No matter how many hundreds and hundreds and hundreds of women pass through the shelter, there will never be two drunks, psychopaths, or obsessive, compulsives alike.

At four o'clock in the afternoon, Betti urinates next to the dumpsters on Lexington Avenue and wipes herself with a scarf and shoves it into her handbag. She sees a shelter worker walking in her direction. She says, "Can I go home with you, Mon, please, thank you very much?"

"You need diapers," the worker says. "Betti, go back and get some diapers to put on yourself."

"Okay, thank you very much." Then she walks back to the shelter a block away where she sits in the basement and smokes until she falls asleep.

The security guards monitor the shelter's Jamaican Queen. When Joanne leaves at night Betti wants to go home with her. Joanne tries to imagine this happening. How Betti would sit on the fabric couch all day long and pee and smoke. That she would need full-time nursing care. What Joanne knows is that Betti will die here at her shelter home. Where have her memories gone? Often, it's the previous lives that the women have lived that keep them spirited. That they want to get back to the other places they were in before they slipped and lost control.

Some of the women have always been mentally ill and they can seem so normal. Recently, one lady was lost to a failed heart. But before she died, even though she was Dennis's client, Joanne knew somethings about the life she led before coming into the shelter system.

Loisaida

Loisaida was obstinate and headstrong. She, like a lot of the women, couldn't internalize the cause-and-effect aspect to life. Dennis knew, and felt plenty, as was evidenced on his face when she died on the street one day on her way to buy a pack of cigarettes and a bottle of orange soda. Dennis also understood that it must have been painful for Loisaida when she thought about her only child whom she hadn't seen in twelve years, nor spoken to in three. Pain was clearly on the daughter's smile and the wetness in the shadows underneath her eyes.

Tony's grandma died, Dennis thought, as he watched two people in Loisaida's family dump her treasures into a black, plastic garbage bag. The grandson held a large basket made of pink-and-white plastic weave up to the light, as if it were transparent. Like him. Like his mother. Trying to look through, squinting his eyes, showing his teeth in a grimace.

Tony stood on a bucket that was left over from soap powder, so he could see the top of his grandma's locker. The same bucket that the clean-up crew had thrown out on a Tuesday, over six months ago. The buckets were discovered as useful containers to empty bladders into during the night by the residents, and with 119 women, about forty of them incontinent, they quickly became the latest fad. But Loisaida screamed and carried on that she needed her bucket because it had valuable things in it.

"What?" the manager asked Dennis when she was questioned on why the bucket was taken and where it could have ended up. "They urinate in the things. Maintenance doesn't have to pick up buckets in the morning that are filled with human waste. The buckets go. The women were told this weeks ago. We don't look inside. We just throw them out."

Hours after it was removed, Loisaida began a search for her bucket with her basket in it. In the basement dumpster, after scrambling through breakfast and lunch, containers of slimy milk, satin blouses from the opulent 1980s, her bucket was found.

She held the contents of the basket up in the air and looked at the workers. Strands of pearls, gold chains in different lengths mixed in with chunky, silver bracelets, dangled in her grasp. There was enough jewelry glowing in the unlit dorm to open a table on Second Avenue and sell the stuff. Loisaida clutched the jewels, the expression on her mouth turned downward.

"These are for my children," she yelled. "Not for the social worker, not for the garbage man, but for my children. You don't touch my things here, over here, ever. I put these box here on my bed," she said, pointing her thumb back at herself. She put her jewels into the pink-and-white basket. She placed the heavier necklaces and bracelets in the bottom, layering them with a felt cloth, then repeated the process with more jewels.

The daughter handed Tony a picture of the grandmother that he knew as Abuela Aida. He gave the same grimace that he had given earlier while looking at her basket. "She looks different here, Mommy," he said, comparing her to pictures that he had seen before of his Abuela when she was healthy and young. The daughter sat on the bed that her mother had slept in, in the shelter where no one in the family knew she was, in the center of the largest cosmopolitan city in the world, in an armory which was built as a fortress against the enemy.

"Abuela was once a beautiful woman with long dark hair, shining brown eyes, and soft tan skin. She wore dresses with many colors like a carnival, and white sandals, when she was at home in the Dominican Republic. She grew flowers in her mother's garden when she was a girl. I think, Tony, that maybe she was just trying to make her own life in the big city like so many women. But she stayed too long and smoked too much and she got older and older until her heart couldn't take care of her any longer."

"Was that the last time you saw her, when she looked that way, Mommy?" referring to his Abuela's youth.

"Yes, it was," she said, picking up her mother's red rubber thongs and placing them under the bed. The shelter surroundings were clean, with a faint smell of turpentine and paint. Depending on where one was standing would determine which was dominant.

"Why didn't she visit our house?"

"Abuela was lost, Tony. She couldn't find us and we couldn't find her."

Dennis looked in on the family as they gathered and picked through Loisaida's things. Deep gray pans, to make cupcakes, that had changed color from having been used, a can opener, one pot. Tools that cooked and fed and conversed a family at some moment in a line of life a long time ago. Rice and beans, plantains, scrambled eggs, still remembered in Loisaida's dreams as the place she was going back to. Her goal was to tell her family where she had been for the last few years after she moved into her own place, which would have been yesterday, Sunday. To take the pot and make rice with saffron. Fill the windows with fresh-cut flowers, each resonating its color in the bright sun, as she imagined it would be. Loisaida spent days and hours in the basement smoking and sleeping and dreaming about the textures in her new home and how her family would be so proud of her. What a beautiful home you have, she heard them say. Smiles on their faces for their Loisaida who had made it at last on her own.

The daughter and Tony picked up the bags with Loisaida's belongings, then walked down the large hall of the 125-year-old building where staff and residents looked for Loisaida in their faces. The daughter whispered: "Tony, don't look at them. Don't give them anything to say about Abuela. Keep your face to yourself. Pretend, Tony, that you are just fine."

When they left, Dennis and Joanne went back to their office. He held it in long enough to shut the door, then he put his head down on his desk and finally let it out. Joanne put her hand on his back. He was sweating, his face was wet from crying.

"They didn't know that she was here. She never let them know where she was. She wanted to surprise them with her new place, but you know what? I believe she still would not have told them where she was," Dennis said.

"Dennis, it was all part of her illness. We can't figure it all out. It's not rational for us. Even the psychiatrists can't figure them out all the time."

Later that day, maintenance bagged her belongings and put them into storage for thirty days. If they are unclaimed, they will be thrown in the garbage.

Through the observation of how one dresses, eats, and keeps her bed area, a lot can be learned. The staff are a team. What the maintenance observes, then letting the social workers know, can be very helpful in a woman's healing. A lot of times the clients think the staff don't see what is going on with them. But they do.

Amy Linn

Amy Linn gets up every day, cleans her body, then disappears into Park Avenue. Her tiny legs hold up her powerful thoughts. Visions that stay close to her like a breathing body that whispers the smell of beer. And sometimes, when she inhales too deeply, she can smell him again. So she concentrates really hard on how much air she takes in. Controlling her intake of it with measured bits of air. In the afternoon, she returns to the shelter and her dorm on the third floor in the armory, where the regiment has maintained a voice for many decades, but not one that interferes with the voices in Amy's head.

Amy's bed is perfectly made, tucked in on all four corners like a military man's. When she realizes that her bed is the way he taught her to make it, she can hear his voice. His silhouette pushes through her life and forward in between her legs and then she smells him all over again. Even with the quick, small, controlled breaths, it doesn't help. He shows up even when there are sixteen other women in the dorm, irregardless of her social worker, who tells her it isn't true. Her social worker tells her it would go away if she would just take her medication, but Amy screams that he is there, and if he would leave her alone, to please leave her alone. "Please do something, make him go away. Why is he here? He don't belong here. Send him away. You lie to me all the time. You say he not here, but he here."

On Thursday, Amy didn't go outside at all. She never left the building, even for a cup of coffee from the local college restaurant. She sat in a stairwell by herself that overlooks the windows that face East 67th Street. She talked softly to her mother in Chinese. Amy started to cry in English and kept saying that she didn't want to do it. "Don't make me do it mother."

Amy's legs speak of little thighs, and she wears black high cut shorts to prove it. She smiles frequently at the staff and is not a problem unless she starts to remember and think about the sheets on her bed. She wonders where the new bedding has gone to. She wants the sheets she was given the first day she came to the shelter. Amy vividly remembers brand-new sheets.

"We never had brand-new sheets," the manager tries to explain. "All the sheets and linens we buy are delivered first to the laundry to be cleaned. Then we get them and they are distributed to all of the clients." Amy lets the manager, and the large halls that are large enough to hold a debutante's party, know exactly how she feels.

"You lie to me. I saw those sheets. I want those sheets. Not old ones. I want new sheets. I am going to report you." The other women sit on the benches in the hall to watch the impending fight. She wants to create chaos and to get the women on her side. She needs to change the sheets all the time. Amy's voice is shrill and loud. The staff want her to talk with her social worker in a corner somewhere in the back. They don't want to use their crisis, intervention techniques that they have been taught in workshops. But the training they have received in domestic violence starts to make sense. The sessions on childhood sexual abuse and the outcome in adults seems to be even more logical, that she could very well have been a victim of one or both of the experiences: the sexual abuse leading to the domestic strife.

Her social worker comes out when the commotion peaks in volume. Energy in the room is high. The molecules in the air tighten up. One pair of eyes follow Amy and they belong to everyone in the room. The social worker begins to tell Amy that she can't scream the way she is. Amy takes her hand and clubs it into a fist and sends it full force into the social worker's face. The clients are alarmed and an aide calls 911.

"I told you he was here," Amy says. "Now I hit him back and now he can cry too." Amy is handcuffed and sent by the police to a mental hospital.

The women who witnessed the attack are scared. Sigrid paces and moves her hands like she is shaking water out of them. Joanne goes over to her and says that Amy will now get the help that she needs. We can't send a client to a mental hospital unless she strikes someone or is determined to be a potentially violent offender. Amy's face is splotched with red. She shakes her head *yes* like she understands. There are times when Joanne believes that Sigrid was sexually abused as a child. Statistics now tell us that the percentage of women who are homeless and were sexually abused as children is high.

Ginger

Ginger's feet are covered in socks and sandals all year long. She won't let the men into the dorm this morning to clean it. They have no business in there, she says. The manager reminds her that she will have to call 911 if she doesn't leave the room. Ginger remains firm. "Call 911," the manager says. Ginger, then, hobbles away.

Ginger has bunions, hammer toes, calluses, and fungus that won't die all over them. Ginger walks too slowly for the other clients who get impatient when she walks in front of them. Donita likes to knock Ginger over when she passes her and act like she didn't do anything. Sloshing past Ginger with a lot of bags so that it always looks like an accident, Donita wants to see Ginger fall down. With her fifteen extra pounds of body muscle and fat, and irregular weave of mental disorders, it is always everyone else that is in the way. Never Donita's.

On a regular day that's like a business day to the sheltered women, because on the weekends and holidays they can stay in their beds all day, if they choose, Ginger and Donita have at least one fight. Molly has one tooth missing in the front of her smile which causes her to whistle when she talks. Then she whistles and sweet-talks the staff when she needs a bit of bleach, not too much. She says, "If you could be so kind as to fill up this itty-bitty cup, I'd be so happy, as there is no one else waiting to do their laundry at this hour, and I figured it'd be a good time for me to get mine done." Ah, yes, cuts into ya like butter. Sweet and soft, no one could resist, except Ginger.

"Why the fuck are ya all fallin' for this cheap glass of wine? Ya all are stupid, stupid peoples workin' here." Ginger, who is constantly in a state of bitterness refuses to see a podiatrist for her feet because she knows that it will go into other problems, like her bad heart, and that they then would have to hospitalize her.

Sadie

The law is very clear: The shelter staff cannot force people to take medication, nor can they force them to seek medical help, unless it is an emergency situation. Sadie attaches herself to specific staff when she needs something. She hates visitors, especially women. She believes that they are trying to throw her out of the shelter. She believes that the government wants to throw all the old ladies onto the streets because they are of no use. Sadie is very ill. The fun part to being around women like Sadie is that sometimes in the middle of her craziness, she makes sense. She has lived a long time and knows a lot.

On a typical day, Sadie finds her way to the stained couches that are slipped into a hallway that face the storage closet and a conference room.

The food from the shelter, she says, makes her sick. She calls herself an old lady, especially when she believes that someone is trying to throw her out into the street and trying to starve her. Sadie believes that she is steps away from being a New York City homeless lady. With the proverbial bag lady look of mismatched clothes and shopping bags—high enough to sit on.

Every few months the New York City firemen come to the shelter to check on violations. Today, Sadie salutes them and smiles. "I'm so glad you're here," she says. "Do you know of a nice place that an old lady like me can live?" The firemen are large to look at. Not at all like the plastic firemen toys that little kids play with. Their uniforms are heavy and black, and have numbers on their hats. She asks: "How do you men do it with all those things on?"

Sadie sits and eats take-out food on the smelly and stained couches and tells the firemen that we are trying to freeze her out of the shelter onto the streets.

"My husband," she begins, "was an engineer and I worked all over the state with him. We had a few houses and lots of dogs. I never wanted children and prayed to God all the time not to let me catch one of those things in me. I was blessed. No children and no heartaches. My mother was a good woman and she raised me well, and if she ever knew what I did on 42nd Street, it would have put her into an early grave. In those days we had little choices, not like women today. We had to get men to survive. Jesus, what I did then. It makes me want to throw up when I think about it."

The firemen want to see the director. One walks away. The remaining fireman tries to be polite. But he walks away too, and Sadie continues to talk as she sees their backs. She stares at the yellow stripes across the shoulders on their black uniforms. "The human body wasn't made for all that stuff," she yells out. "It was made for one-on-one. We are not supposed to have all the partners that we want to."

Sadie holds onto her head. It is starting to hurt again. When it starts, she goes back in time to the 1940s and 1950s. She hears the music of Benny Goodman, "In the Mood," and she is raven-haired again and on 42nd Street. She sees the firemen as sailors. Sadie shakes her hips from side to side. She waves her hand over her head. Her right arm that is blown up twice its size, slips out from the scarf that she had it wrapped in. She tries to tiptoe in her orthopedic shoes. "Hey sailor," she yells out, "do you want to dance?" Sadie's perfect denture smile looks sinister. "I wonder why they won't come back?" Then in a whisper, she says: "They never do."

Theresa has just told Joanne that she will be moving out of the shelter. She slumps down into the foldable chair. Her knees are pushed together, her head tilts downward:

During most of their meetings she avoids eye contact with Joanne. She has returned to speaking while showing only the side of her head.

"I can get a place by Frances," she says.

Joanne was hoping that Frances would express herself more to Theresa, now that she is moving out. "Theresa, you and Frances are different people. You need different living situations," Joanne says.

"I can live like Frances."

"Yes, you can live like Frances, but you need more support than she does. Frances is moving into a single-room occupancy building. You need residential care for adults. You could live very nicely in a facility where you could be with other adults, yet have perhaps a room to yourself." She then asked Joanne if that was where the old lady went to. The other unofficial staircase monitor who had chronic diarrhea.

"No, she went to a nursing home facility. You don't need to be in a nursing home, either. It's good that you are asking questions and that you are starting to see yourself in a different housing situation. I want to help you get a place to live that will be comfortable and that will work to help you with your special needs," Joanne said.

Joanne understands that Theresa wants a place to live in like the one her daddy threw her out of so many years ago. She wants to return to the southern safety of a large family. She also wants to be with Frances, who has always been very nurturing to her.

#   #   #

In the sweltering days of Indian summer, the clients lie against the walls in shaded corners. The dining room is without lights, turned off to keep the sweat away.

The fans blow hot air around, insulting their pores. The staff make the calls on the environment. They continue to keep the clients in suspense about the renovations that could alleviate some of them from the torments from the hot and cold weather.

The large dorm is not habitable in the summer. Only for the flies that breed in dirty underwear and opened jars of cold cream. Dead larva, from flies, darken the crevices of the twist caps. Like the flies, the workers, can be confused by the sweet smell.

Some of the women want to see the heat as an enemy who wants to get even with them. It's something they did wrong. Why do they deserve such an evil fate? The staff are also accused of causing it to force them out of the shelter. Some of the women will say "they are trying to get rid of us. They follow us to see where we go and to know what we do. They want us out so the others can get in."

Theresa begs Joanne for a short sleeved shirt, size ten, so her arms can be exposed, bare, in the dusty halls. Theresa sits on a leather seat perspiring into a dimension that can be compared, and equaled, to hell.

Feliciana sleepwalks with her lover. Joanne stops her, to sit her down outside the dorm in the hall. Joanne keeps her still, away from the staircases that are grand, with curling banisters and wide enough to fit a room into and to fill it with twenty women and twenty beds and dressers that would hold their clothing.

Feliciana's eyes are open, and Joanne stays by her side until she goes back to sleep. During the day, when the staff run around the halls and into the rooms, replenishing the supplies and moping up the floors, Feliciana sits and talks about her lover. How is it, she wonders, that she can dream about him and yet he is never near?

And in Joanne's own private thoughts, she wonders about the same thing. Where has her lover gone to? How is it that she can dream about him and he, like Feliciana's lover, is far away from her? How can enchantment be one-sided? Joanne's loneliness weaves into Feliciana's and blends with threads of familiarity crossing over. And so Joanne tells her that he is not far away. Events and throttles of life, jutting forward, and at times, inclining upward or downward. But because he is in her heart he is never far away. That the love she had with him will always stay the same.

Then Feliciana takes her gray-and-black hair and sticks it up, off from her neck, with a bobby pin. She lies back in her bed and tells Joanne not to use her name. Never to speak her name out loud. The words Joanne uses to comfort her now become the words of the enemy. She has bounded into the memory of the abuse that her lover insisted she have.

"Mio, mio, mio," she chants, hiding her face into her knees. Her aqua pedal pushers have stains from her tears.

Monday, September 20, 1999

It is Monday morning and all have returned to work. Even though they have twenty-four-hour coverage, the weekends at the shelter are different than the weekdays. The women also get the weekends off, and are allowed to stay in the dorms and sleep, and to go back and forth as many times as they choose.

Dennis and the director rub elbows for a few seconds. The director runs and gets on the elevator with them. Dennis holds the door open and begins to tell him about Ava and the breakthrough that she had earlier that morning. The door wasn't willing to wait to hear about Ava. It banged against his hand that he had positioned outward like a traffic cop. Dennis is an emotional man. He fans his arms around when he speaks, holds onto an unlit cigarette, and keeps pushing his eyeglasses up the bridge of his nose.

"Oh, it was so sad," he started.

The director took a deep breath, looked up at him briefly, then walked off the elevator when it got to his floor. Then he said, "So what happened?"

"Ava finally spoke to me. I mean really spoke to me. She sat and cried. I couldn't believe it. It was so good. She cried about her mother and how she said that she never wanted her. And when she was growing up in Jamaica her mother made her wash the floors all the time and she beat her with the end of a broom. She said her mother also told her that she had her because she had no choice and hated her for it. It was terrible. But it was so good that she told me. And God, the tears…so sad."

The director was arriving at work for the first time after losing his younger sister to a driving accident. He had started to feel warm from the heat in the building. His pants felt tight around his waist and that annoyed him.

"How do you know that she isn't lying?"

Dennis looked disappointed. Not a disappointment that he hadn't considered Ava's story a lie on his own, but that the director was questioning him on that issue. "I suppose I was just glad to have her sit for a moment, make eye contact with me, and want to talk to me at all."

"Well then, that's the way it goes. Sometimes we just have to accept our losses. She lost her childhood. Who hasn't?"

Dennis caught his insensitivity and gasped. The director had just buried a sister the past week and was at work this morning out of duty. "I'm sorry. How are you doing?"

"She's out of her pain. Dead. Gone into the cold ground now, separating us for good. But you know what, Dennis? She lived. She was an artist who lived her life as she wanted to. I always admired how she lived exactly as she wanted and didn't give into social mores like so many of us do. So now we have Ava, who is seventy-something years old and she still cares about what her crazy mother did to her when she was a kid."

"It takes as long as it takes. You know that. For some of us it does take a life-time," Dennis said.

The director walked into his office past the line of clients waiting for lunch. "Good morning everyone. I'm glad to be back. Everyone behaving themselves...I hope..."

He needed to cry, too. Sometimes his own life was filled with gaps and unexplained feelings, but here he was dedicating his life to a shelter filled with women who "lost it" a long time ago. He dropped his bags onto the floor, his jacket over the back of his chair. Dennis sat across from him, waiting for more feedback.

"It's real good that Ava has cried about her mother. You know as well as I that she is going to use every trick in the book to keep from moving on to permanent housing," he said. "She's the type. Been to three other shelters over the past twelve years."

"She's terrified of being on her own," Dennis said.

"I know that. But you have to keep *her needs* in focus. The treatment she needs to get from you is not supposed to be that introspective right now. She's entangling you so you can become a part of her, and it's just too much. She has to plan move out! We had a place for her and she just refused to go. She can continue with the one-on-one type of therapy when she leaves but for now, I want you to keep pushing her into the housing issue. Let her cry, but let her move too."

Dennis just sat and looked at the director. His face and impatience told him that he wanted to be alone. Stanley picked himself up and walked out. The director went to the window on his door to close the blinds. Stanley looked back at him through the glass and their eyes locked. The director's were wet. Then he turned the wand and closed the blinds for the rest of the day.

People like to play games. They also like to win at games. Bingo is a really popular game at the shelter. The recreation specialist, Evelyn, sets up a bingo game once a week during the daytime for the women. They can win prizes like powder, shampoo, stockings, batteries, nail polish, petroleum jelly, and slippers. They also get jealous of each other, coveting the prizes for themselves. This is a good place to enforce some basic rules and to instill socialization skills.

"Bingo," Ruby yelled to Evelyn.

"You got a cross on the card or an "X"? Miss Ruby?"

"Why you always think I'm waistin' your time? Come lookie here. I got all the buttons straight across the board right down the line." Ruby grabbed her plastic grocery bags, pulling them close to her as Evelyn stood up and walked over. Her bags were layered one inside the other three, four, five of them. Stuffed with pieces of notebook paper containing journal type notes, tethered balls of toilet paper, four different kinds of hand cream, used bars of soap wrapped in toilet paper, and some Christmas cards that she had been meaning to send to her brother and sister and their children as soon as she could get some stamps.

Evelyn knew what Ruby was holding onto and why she wanted her bingo card to be the winner. The big prize this week was a large plastic bottle of aloe vera, hand cream with a free hand pump. All the bingo players wanted that hand cream.

"That's not bingo, Miss Ruby. The first game has to be a cross," Evelyn put two fingers together that looked like a letter "T, or an 'X. Not *across,* but one cross sign."

Evelyn went back to rolling the numbers and calling them out: "B-9, G-46, O-75…if I am going too fast for anyone let me know…B-10, I-20, B-14, N36, B-7." A bingo ball with a number on it fell out of the basket and rolled under the table. A few of the women scrambled to the ground for it. A lot of them are grandmothers—women with their babies on their minds, babies out of sight with miles between the day they came through the birth canal and into the *real* world. Hair long and gray, some with rubber curlers, imperfect, scraggly, parted hair, tinted by at-home hair-dye kits: poor hair rarely brushed by its owner, mostly combed by a friend or a partner.

Evelyn continued: "N-39, N-41, B-11. Want me to sing?"

"Bingo!" a little white-haired Jewish lady yelled.

"Damn," Ruby yells. "*They* always win."

The little Jewish lady came up and took batteries for her radio as her prize. Ruby is relieved the hand cream is still there. She felt her heart race; she wanted that cream.

"Come on baby," Evelyn sings, "Twist and Shout. Or did we do the Jerk? 0-70, G-46, O-51, 0-57, N-36, B-15…"

"Bingo," Ruby yells.

"You ain't got no bingo," Brenda yells back.

"Come on up," Evelyn says. "And don't stand behind me. Get in front."

She checks Ruby's card. It's bingo for Ruby. Ruby grabs the hand cream and leaves the room.

Out by the bathroom where the tough city girls hang out on the steps and the garbage can tops, Sonia waits. Her teeth, hellified points glaring downward at the cracks of her smile, her eyeballs appearing like brown peas behind her eyeglasses, her smile looks like a six-year-old's.

"You ain't never gettin' a job the way you look," Lena says to Sonia as the smoke from her cigarette leaves her mouth with her words.

"You don't know that. Why you always so *neg a tive?* Always so negative." Sonia walked away from Lena, washed her hands in one of the twelve sinks, then sat on a chair in the doorway of the bathroom. She looked out to where Lena was sitting and focused her attention on Lena's legs. They were long, and crossed at the knees. Lena's voice was deep even before she started to smoke when she became a bartender in 1978. Her face was big and broad at the cheekbone, and forehead. Lena was at least six feet tall. One hesitated to ask just how tall she was, at least to her face, as she was so tall and deep throated, it was obvious that something was up with her. Once in a while, one of the other clients would tell her that she was really a man. Sonia had no problem saying it when she was high or crashing.

Sonia got up and sat on the garbage can with her arms folded so she could support that cigarette puffin' cloud that hung in the doorway to the bathroom. She let her feet stick out a bit too far so that when the women needed to use the bathroom they had to ask her first to please move her legs. She would do so with her beady black eyes staring back at the bathroom user. What she wanted to do was to barricade all the women out of the bathroom and watch them pee on the floor. Sonia laughed out loud every time she thought about the possibility. Pee all over the floor. Maintenance men scrambling with disinfectant to clean it up. Aides spraying the air with room deodorizer while shaking their heads and holding their noses. But then she heard Lena say something. Lena stood up and said the words loud so she was goddam sure that Sonia heard her.

"Sonia looks like a little pig and she ain't never goin' to get no job with no teeth in her head."

"Oh yeah," Sonia yelled, jumping off the garbage can with her cigarette in her hand, "What do you know? You really a man and everybody know it. And I saw your man. He really a bitch, and everyone know that too."

"At least I got a man. You have no one at all. What you got is a fat little ass and no teeth. Why you always laughing and smiling and showing those gums. You are disgusting."

Sonia stood her ground and said, "Come and say it right here to my face, you testosterone bag of shit." Lena walked toward Sonia, who was now standing on the bathroom steps. Towering over a fat, round head, Lena looked down at Sonia, who was breaking a waterline of sweat on her forehead. Lena stared downward, long and hard, until her eyes crossed. They were in each other's safe space that boundary of undefined air around the self that extends about eighteen inches around, and then they just laughed. The aides let out a collective sigh.

"You got a light?" Sonia asked showing her gums.

This shelter is located in a landmark building, which is an armory, like a few other shelters in the city. On the main floor is a large, closed-in area, the drill floor, that takes up one half a block. The armory rents it to art shows for forty weeks out of the year. The shelter, therefore, during those shows, must share the only elevator in the building with art dealers and buyers from all over the world. Occasionally, a ride on the Otis is more than one could ever imagine a fifteen-second ride should be. One day there were two visitors: a well-dressed woman in a red woolen suit smelling of Bloomingdale's perfume, and a man. Her makeup made her look porcelain, her teeth perfectly white with beautiful dental caps. They could have been husband and wife, close to each other in some way, because she whispered to him that there was a stench in the elevator. Everyone heard her, even though she did try to muffle her words, they could still hear her.

The manager couldn't smell anything because she had been working in the place for so long that unless someone had just taken a shit, and it was fresh, to her it didn't stink. The manager was alarmed at the callousness of the visitor in the elevator. Mostly the elevator is used for the shelter residents and staff on the two shelter floors.

The manager didn't care where the woman came from or what her goal was. She was more concerned about how the clients felt about themselves, and was really angry when the sweet-smelling, perfectly coiffed woman made that comment.

The air was tight. No one looked up at the elevator door or watched the floor numbers light up.

Theresa, Sadie, and a new client were on the elevator with the manager and the two visitors. Sadie was looking for the firemen, as she had an idea about fire safety for them. She told the manager that she wanted to tell them something very important, and could she help her find them.

"I think they left the building," the manager said to Sadie, not wanting to talk at all with the strangers in the elevator. She nursed the fantasy of smacking the visitors in their heads and watching them fix their hair after their pounding from her angry hand. She didn't want them to hear anything from the ladies. The manager wanted to protect "her women" from cruelty. Ordinarily, she hated any display of a "we against them" mentality, but in these few moments she definitely felt a division.

The elevator stopped at every floor in the building. Sadie looked at the manager and then at the other two clients and lastly at the two visitors. The woman was looking at the ceiling, but Sadie stared at her. Sadie's eyes got watery. Then she said: "I apologize for what I am about to do." She then straddled her legs, lifted up her skirt to her knees, and pissed on the floor. The puddle wasn't very large, as her bladder was old and frail and couldn't hold much for very long. The visiting lady started to cry. The man, who the manager now realized was the visiting lady's husband, pushed her face into his suit jacket.

"Get me out of here," the visiting lady said.

"You're a disgrace to women," the man said to Sadie as he continued to cradle his wife's face in his chest.

Sadie took her fat arm out of the sling that it was in, waved it up over her head, and sang, "I'm Looking Over A Four Leaf Clover..." and danced in her pee at the same time.

The manager looked at Sadie and in a clear, loud voice said: "Is that what you were going to show the firemen, Sadie?"

"...that I overlooked before..."

Rita

Rita opens her mouth and looks in the mirror; she sees a dog. He growls and shows his front white teeth. He is getting ready to bite her. The way Spy, her German Shepherd, did when he heard her coming home just before she opened the door to the apartment she shared with him. She says: "I see Spy in my mouth. He be barkin' at me each time I look into the mirror. He comin' closer to the mirror an' soon he gonna be out of me."

Rita lived with her mother once in time in a rent-controlled apartment for forty-five years, until her mother was six months dead. The landlord pushed his face and fancy, attorney-bred papers into court when Rita could hardly walk. Her hip pained her so badly that she wanted to die, causing her to miss two court appearances. She froze all her feelings inside herself when the notices came from the courthouse on Center Street in downtown New York City. So she stayed on the fat chair that her mother died in and waited for the marshals who *did* come to take her away at last, right to the front of her building with everything she owned, including the chair.

Two neighbors in her building took turns taking care of her, but she started to act like her mother, whom they remembered. They got together one day, and talked about Rita and how hard she was to take care of, and then they called the city welfare office. At first Rita cried and said to the city people that she didn't do anything wrong to anybody; why, she kept asking, are you mad at me?

Rita was escorted from the intake shelter in the Bronx to the private shelter in the nice side of New York City. She walked off the elevator, and even with a cane, she had to drag her leg because of her hip. She had the look on her face like many of the women when they first arrive. Like she was funneled through a hole after the wash/spin cycle in a washing machine. Who the hell were all these other women that were very sick and nasty-looking? Ten women sat on the hall benches that were military landmark furniture and watched the new arrival. They stared her down and looked at her unbendable feet, her stiff legs, and the raincoat she was wearing in the twenty-eight-degree temperature. Her eyes were gray and she looked around for a mirror to see if the dog was still with her. She pulled back toward the transitioning worker and said: "I'm goin' home. I got a home. I don't belong here. Look at all these crazy people. Please get me out of here."

The intake social worker in the shelter saw the abyss in Rita's eyes. She smiled at her. "It's going to be okay. Are you hungry? Have you eaten anything today? It looks like you need a chair."

Rita looked down at her feet and thought they were her mother's. Her hair was sticking out of her baseball cap like raggedy pieces of white cardboard. She took the chair when the social worker brought it over, sat down, and let out a sigh.

"There's a dog in my mouth," Rita said to the worker, opening it really wide and pointing inward with her finger.

"Ask him if he is hungry," the social worker said. Rita sat for a moment then shook her head, yes. For a brief moment, the social worker could see the dog, too.

Rita looked into the large dining room and saw a chair like the one she owned until the marshals threw her out onto the street. She got up and caned herself over to the chair that was huge and brown and very old. Now, however, she could hear Spy bark. He barked the way he used to when he met a stranger and didn't want the stranger to go near Rita. Rita felt safe that Spy was protecting her. She told him to be quiet, that he could go to sleep, and that no one was going to hurt her. But he didn't quiet down, so she found her Walkman and turned up the music. Rita could no longer hear Spy, but dreamt about the job she once had as a secretary and the good feelings she had about her boss. How she felt when he kissed her, and that she was married to him, until her mother broke it up. Spy barked louder and louder, snapping her out of the dream. Rita was angry and spat at the social worker who was now at her side, telling her to go somewhere upstairs to sleep.

"There's a goddam dog in me and you woke him up and now he won't stop barking," Rita said.

The longer Joanne worked at the shelter, the more tolerant she become of the mentally ill. She was fascinated by their ability to seem so normal, while they are so challenged. Everyday routines are either not established within them, or they are so obsessed with routine and narcissistic with their own lives only, that they cannot live. The social workers defined functional as being able to fit into everyday society and live a so-called normal life. Joanne knows people in her own family that are supported by family members, and friends that are really just as ill as the women here, but because no one has given up, or discovered them yet, they remain in the society we call mainstream.

Ava

Ava was a showgirl. In a time during the 1950s when a dab of mascara and a pinch of the cheeks was enough to make a girl pretty before she walked into the casting office. Long before computerized visions of adjusted noses and hair color were available to the waiting beauty, Ava made her bones and honed her craft by herself. No one helped her. And what a beauty she must have been when she was younger.

Her face structure was still a giveaway to where she found her power. And now the years have passed for Ava, like they do for everyone else. She now keeps the cap on her head to hide the balding. The light is dimmed alluding to her beauty, that it is still with her. The beauty has not gone, but has deepened with wrinkles and pain. The raging tide in her was most likely there when she was younger and lively, but harder to see. Our Ava, a master nurturer for old ladies, feeling capable and young just by taking care of the old and frail.

Our star of the shelter world, who folds her bed over three times on a good day, to keep the staff from looking at her any closer. The lights of the stage that once gave her brilliance to the audience and claimed the applause, she now hides from twenty-five watt bulbs.

Tall and spry, she runs around with the energy of a starlet. She lights up cigarettes with the other old ladies who can only sit on the benches all day long. They congregate and decide that this is a shelter where secrets are kept. That we are out to get them is good for their brains. It keeps them thinking and fluid. The group whispers about the horrendous staff who take from them what they want when the clients aren't looking.

Ava, our mother in residence who comforts the sleeping matrons who snooze in the halls from large doses of medicine from psychiatrists, as a long-time resident who recalls the old days in the shelter and is a walking historian of a fore life in this culture.

Ava loves to hate the staff. She shoots her daffy expression and overly made up face into our calm gatherings. She flies into today's community meeting, insisting they reassemble the metal detector. Knives and guns are coming into the shelter and she wants it stopped. Her life is in jeopardy. The lives of sleeping, overly medicated women are in jeopardy. "We could be raped," she yells. "We could be murdered." Some of the clients nod their heads in agreement; some just listen, so old, their spines don't line up with the back's of the chairs, so curved, their digestion is challenged.

Theresa stands in the doorway, listening to Ava. Ava wants a woman to run the shelter. "Men cannot be trusted. They lie and they are leeches. They wait for us to sleep before they make their real rounds.

"I also believe," she continues, "that the FBI is watching us from the hole in the ceiling; I saw the wires before they were colored yellow. My report is with my attorney against this shelter, as this shelter is stealing all of my money out of my locker every time I leave the dorm. Let me finish; that is why I want a complete copy of my records, they are my records and I don't see why I have to write a request to get information about myself. No, I will not work with Dennis, that thing you call a social worker. This man has no experience whatsoever in life and how the hell can he tell me how to live my life? I am moving out of here as soon as you give me back all of the money you took from my locker. Why am I the target, I leave nothing on my bed, it's stripped down, like a woman, I might add, every day. And no, I can't get up and out onto the street by

eight AM every day because I know I don't have to. I have
the right to stay as long as I want to. Dennis was asking me
about my father, now what does my father have to do with
my living in this shelter? My father has been dead for
almost 50 years. He was a hard-working man who would
put any so-called man today to shame. Not a soul in this
room could do the work he did as a farmer. So what are
you going to do about the FBI in the ceiling?"

Everyone in the community meeting quieted and looked
at each other. The manager spoke up: "The hole in the
ceiling is from the chandelier that almost fell down. We are
waiting for the state to come and reattach the light. There
are some wires exposed in different colors, but the different
colors are to caution the handler of the wires as to how to
use them.

"No one has the key to your locker but you. You get a
lock and it has two keys. They are not with anyone else but
each of you."

"Well how do you account for the new Pepsi cans? The
new design is because we are being watched, and I urge all
of you not to buy these cans unless you don't care who is
watching you. Yes, that's right, on each and every can in
the new color blue is the truth. They are watching us. And
my lawyer is looking at my report right now."

The manager continued: "The new Pepsi cans are a
design by the Pepsi Cola Company to enhance their
marketability. Pepsi Cola has nothing to do with the
shelter. They are simply cans that are put into the soda
machine by the vendor. There is no connection between the
FBI and this shelter."

Ava's pageboy-styled hair flounces under her baseball
cap. She has no teeth and it is a strain to listen to her words.
A bit deeper-throated and she could sound like an imitation
of Daffy Duck. Her coat is buttoned up to her collar and
she wears gloves and a scarf all the time. Ava shuts off the

lights on the wall where she sits in the large hall. She takes out her make up and opens the compact and views her reflection. Rouge is added to her wrinkled face, lipstick is reapplied, she brings her brows up to a surprised look flickering her lashes while separating them with a mascara brush. Under her cap is a white strip of paper that circles around her head.

"The radiation from the building is seeping through," she tells Peggy who is nodding off to sleep after all the excitement from the visitors. "You need to have one for your head, too. Why let them take your mind? They are trying to kill us here. I have seen the men come in on the fourth floor, onto the roof, pretending to deliver vegetables to us."

Ava takes a few napkins folds them for Peggy and places them on Peggy's head. Peggy has fallen asleep under the light in the hallway, her body returning to its slumped over form. Ava covers Peggy's shoulders with one of the new sweaters she was given from her visitors. She looks over to see who is watching her. Sigrid is.

A wandering figure in the old hall, she watches, and speaks to herself. Mandy manages the space around her and controls the bench area where she sits. Sigrid continues to be equally as frazzled as Mandy. Sigrid wants to use Donita's cart to go to the store. The Genovese drug store has a sale on napkins and cups. She wants to catch the sale. To horde the items to satisfy her sense of safety. Thomasina throws her head up into the air, as if needing to see beyond her diminutive stature.

When Thomasina first talks to you, it isn't hard to see her mental illness. She is without balance in her phrasing. She just starts talking when she sees you, talking about anything that she wants. How she never had sex for money; how she is not homeless because she was beaten, but homeless because "they" took everything away from her.

She boldly watches all those around her. She desires friendliness, yet she is unfriendly.

Donita runs away with her cart. No one is clean enough for her to use her cart. She would use disinfectant until her brain stunk of it to clean away the demon bacteria. She wraps plastic around the handle and squirrels the cart under her bed, hoping and praying that the staff didn't see it.

#   #   #

Joanne is exhausted from the women today. They have fought and screamed. She has listened and comforted and wandered with her soul around their minds. Her day has been spent cornering their fears long enough so they can unleash them. She lives the process of being there, of having no judgment, of being the authority figure who never criticizes.

Joanne goes in one direction to tend to Kathy. Kathy has been very quiet today. Perhaps she, too, like Theresa, is remembering that Frances is leaving soon. Maybe she is discomforted at the idea of someone leaving and another coming in. Donita peers out of the dorm without her cart. She wants Joanne to notice. She walks over to Joanne and stands behind she and Kathy, as if she is waiting on line for her turn. Step right up and get a helping of your trusted social worker. She is here for you only.

Donita will complain, no doubt, that she had to clean the shower with her bare hands. The scent of a demented woman's feces has haunted her all day. She tells Joanne all about it, and wants to talk and talk and talk about it. She wants Joanne to make sure the demented woman, Betti, doesn't do it again. Donita, obsessed, has no sympathy for the demented. They have to be considerate of others. Staff secretly think that Donita would serve all of them well if she would move out. How they pray some days for her to just go away. To stop the outward chatter; the endless compulsion. The mind entanglements that wear a day staff of twenty-two into migraines.

Joanne breathes deeply and turns around to Donita: "I will see you when I get done with Kathy."

"It'll just be a minute," she Donita says.

Joanne ignores Donita's request and turns around to continue with Kathy, who asks for so little, but she is walking quickly around the wall that leads to the staircase. Theresa follows Joanne as she walks after Kathy. Kathy sits on a chair, crosses her arms, and refuses to look at Joanne.

"I know you're angry with me, I'm sorry. Can we continue now?" Joanne says.

There is no room for client transition today. No room to go from one to another with a breath in between. There are only spots and clusters of chaos. It's like working in a nursery and all the babies need to be fed at once and there aren't enough nurses. At first Kathy refuses to move. Her breathing falls quiet. The hall for a moment is lit with the sun from the street. They appreciate the glow. It gives optimism to their session. Kathy wants to talk to Joanne about Jim, the lover that left her years ago. The artist who never returned after her husband finally found out about their affair.

"I want you to call me Mrs. DeMaio from now on," she begins.

"That's fine. I can do that," Joanne says.

"That's who I really am. I am Mrs. DeMaio. That's my real name."

"I know that it's your last name, but you want me to call you that instead of Kathy?"

"Yes. That's my name. It's proper. All the other whores here are nasty and filthy and I can't be like them. I was never like them and I will be called from now on by my proper name, or I will not answer."

Joanne was glad that Kathy was talking and that she was thinking. That she was making a decision was a miracle. Her prejudice was an over-compensation for some other deficits that she probably had ingrained into her when she was a kid; it is just too fearful for her to make those changes yet. Kathy is also deeply guilt ridden from leaving her children when she left her husband. Calling her Mrs. DeMaio will now help her feel less common, Joanne realizes. She needs to feel better about herself. Even if it is an illusion. Joanne lets her make all the decisions she wants, as long as she doesn't hurt anyone else.

By the time Joanne leaves the hallway where Mrs. DeMaio flips from one stage to another, Donita and Theresa are shouting at each other. Frances approaches the two. But Frances is smelling of alcohol this afternoon. Joanne steps backward to look her over. She is calm and actually good at focusing on the women. Donita is impatient.

"You're drunk," Donita says. "You smell like a fucking drunk. How dare you come over to us. Get away from me."

Frances wants to hold onto her dignity. "I am not drunk," she says. "You need to look at your own life and not think of mine. When are you getting out of here?"

Joanne puts her arm onto Frances's shoulder and whispers, "Let's talk."

They walked into the back office where we escaped the late lunch delivery and the smoking chameleons that wait on the benches for the time to tap, tap away.

"You smell of alcohol. What's going on?" Joanne begins.

"I don't know why I got drunk, I just did. I like it. It's my life and I can do what I want. I'm leaving soon, in a few days, and I want to celebrate life and the women here who will never get out like me."

"You are not responsible for the other women here. Let us do what we have to do with them."

"I know that they are not my problem."

"So let them alone. Don't try to be their social worker. You have enough of your own life to take care of. Don't worry about theirs."

"So who are you to do this work here, with all this going on? Who are any of you to tell any of us what to do?"

"Have you made changes since you have been here?"

"Some. I've made some changes."

"Good! Now let us take care of the other women. We are trained to do this work. Trust me on this one."

"I don't want to trust you anymore. I just want to leave here."

"And you are. And you have done very well for yourself here. Do you think you will miss the shelter? You can always come and visit us. You can stop by and have lunch or dinner. You are always welcome to visit," Joanne said.

"I just don't know what to do with myself when I get there, you know to the new place that I am supposed to be so excited about."

"Clean it up," Joanne said. "I'll help you." Then they both laughed.

How could it be easy for her? It's not easy for anyone to lose their home and have to live temporarily with one-hundred-and-eighteen other roommates. One-hundred-and-nineteen women, one-hundred-and-nineteen different stories. No two are alike. Each woman comes with her own delicate past and hopes for a different life.

"I don't know if I can make it on my own anymore. I'm so scared to live by myself, to take care of myself."

"Of course you are scared. Who wouldn't be? But I believe you can do it. I believe that you can make it. Just one foot in front of the other, each day. That's all any one of us can do. Everyone gets scared from changes and different things that come our way in life. You are not alone in feeling this way. I am just wondering what you think and how you feel? Do you ever separate the two? Do you think about the differences between both? Do you think there are differences between them?"

Then Frances wiped her eyes. She thought for a second; then she got quiet. "I think I can do it, but I feel queasy about it," she said.

"When you feel that it's uncomfortable, stay with the feeling, try to place it to where it began. You don't have to do it now with me," Joanne said, "maybe you will continue with a therapist when you leave here. It would be so good for you."

Joanne thought about the women who had left and how so many of them passed away within' months or a few years. So many have preexisting health issues that they choose to ignore even after the shelter was able to evaluate them, and offer them medical care. A lot have hypertension and high cholesterol from poor diets and genetic factors. She was sure that a few died because they wanted to, and had just given up on life, as well.

But Joanne had to have high hopes for Frances. If she didn't, then she would be able to tell whenever Joanne told her that she could make it out there, that she was lying. She had to believe that they still had a chance at life when they left the shelter.

Hazel

How easy it was to remember Hazel whenever Frances and Joanne met. Frances's impending departure reminded her so much of Hazel who was an absolute favorite of hers. If she could have taken her home with her she would have. Joanne cherished that lady.

Hazel was a Mid-western lady who, in her late sixties, had to run away from her husband because he beat her. During a weekly meeting in the nostalgia group at the shelter, she shared what her life was like as a young girl on a farm a long time ago. There was no need to go to school after she turned twelve, even though she wanted to continue her education. Hazel wanted to be a cheerleader. And she dreamt of moving to Chicago where she could be a librarian because of her love for books. But she was needed on the farm to take care of the cows and chickens to help her folks so they could make a living.

"Those were just the way times were during the depression and there was no choice. Either work the farm or leave it. We had large pitchforks that, Lordy Jesus if you didn't watch out when daddy was pitchin', you could get yourself jabbed. Not that he meant it, but farmin' was tough work, unlike today. Everyone worked then."

Joanne met Hazel on the first day she arrived at the shelter. Her eyes were calling out for a connection and Hazel seemed motherly. She was a big woman who wore skirts all the time with clear stockings. She had tired lines across her face like she didn't sleep well. She showed up at the shelter door, a homeless lady with a few plastic bags.

Joanne introduced herself to Hazel and asked if she was okay, did she need anything? Hazel had the twilight-zone expression on her face that said: Where am I? How did I get here? This was one of the few ladies that passed through the shelter that wasn't mentally ill or substance abusing. It's never been a crime to be a lost soul, yet Hazel looked guilty. Hazel had a sadness that was deep inside her-so deep in fact, that it came out in her face because there was so much in there.

For the next few weeks, whenever Hazel saw Joanne, she would watch her walk into the room, across the room, until she left the room. Joanne always said hello; she always wanted to get closer to Joanne and into her life, but it was a call she couldn't make as she was not Hazel's social worker. Therefore, she had to do my best to maintain some distance and professionalism, even though her heart kept saying get closer to Hazel, get to know her. For some reason, like a lot of things that happen in life, she just liked her. Maybe it was the effort she had made in life that came through in her essence. Maybe, too, it was the sincerity she had when she asked for something because she really needed it. Hazel was humble and loving, and in the nostalgia group-the last one before she left the shelter-she told the women that she had a daughter once who was killed in a car accident. "She was a school teacher and I was so proud of her. I put her through college with extra farmin' money and made aprons and pies for sellin' at the market on Saturdays. She was teachin' sixth graders at the time, and I was goin' to go live with her, but then she had the accident."

The group leader said that it was sad, and for the group to sit and say nothing for a few minutes. Then Hazel said that she was happy today because she had found a place to live, and how helpful the housing specialist and everyone in the shelter had been to her.

Hazel was overjoyed on her moving day. She couldn't wait to get situated and go to the famous midtown library-the large one with the cement lions out front on Fifth Avenue and 42nd Street.

101

It was during a community meeting, about eight months later, that it was announced that Hazel was in an accident. She was hit by a car while walking on Broadway in the theater district and was killed. Even now, Joanne's heart still sinks when she remembers Hazel. She wishes that she had allowed herself to get closer to her. Breaking the rules is the missing element in human services, where paperwork, boundaries, and staid language like "appropriateness," "out of control," and "speak to your social worker," can interfere with caring for people from the heart.

Denise

There are the temporaries of the temporary. When Joanne meets a new client for the first time, she wonders, alone, what happened to this lady? How did she end up here? And she thinks of the social sicknesses that they get caught up in. Joanne remembers that they are human and, like her they are women. They have love lives, they went to school, had crushes on boys when they were growing up. They listened to the radio and danced the latest moves to songs of their time. They wanted to win the lottery and marry a good man. They wanted their children to be safe and secure. They wanted the picture-postcard of a perfect life.

She didn't believe that any one of them ever woke up in their lives and said I want to live in a shelter when I grow up. Or that I want to be a drug addict or to be a psychotic, dependent, difficult woman who pisses on myself and is sleeping on a 34-inch-wide cot waiting to die.

Denise hasn't been in this shelter that long, but as anyone can see, she was once a tall, pretty woman. Her eyes, now, however, are usually half-closed for most of the time that she is vertical. Denise nods out standing up, believing that if she stands no one will think that she has *picked-up* or that she is *using*. Her language has been permanently changed and her tone is now a wining, nasal, monotone voice that is consistent with the way drug addicts talk. Her speech has been changed so that when she isn't high she still sounds like a "druggie." Denise is aware of it, and while she is a clean woman and tries to be soft-spoken and is always picking the lint off her clothes, ironing her jeans, and washing her hair, she is street. At 58-years-old, she is a grandmother. But "granny" is not home baking cookies and sending Valentine's Day cards to her daughter's children. She shamefully cries on her birthday as it has been unrecognized by the shelter and she has been forgotten by her family. Her large eyes are half closed today, frozen like a frog's to a bulgy and tired look. Denise says she wants to get clean. That she wants her life back. But the staff know, that the only life she misses is the one she had when she took drugs on a daily basis from her own apartment not caring who was there. She was baby-sitting one time for her grandchildren and a friend came over to free base with her. The kids were curious during the commercials of "The Simpsons" and wandered into Granny's bedroom and saw a lit candle: It looked more intriguing than Bart and Lisa. Upon reaching for the candle, it then tipped over and Granny's bed went on fire. The kids were overcome with smoke before they could grab the doorknob. The grandson died. The two granddaughters lived. But that was the last time she saw them, and she can't remember lighting the candle, or who was in the apartment with them. That was nine years ago, and Denise has been on the streets ever since. In and out of shooting galleries, junkie homes, and apartments. No one in the family wants her anymore.

She gets lit up more and more, unable to break out of the numbness. The shelter folks know when she isn't high, as she starts to feel and becomes very sad. Alone, she will sit on the bathroom bench staring off into space, her large eyes lonely and watery. She is unafraid to stare back into the eyes of the worker when she is asked how she is doing.

"Not too good today. I don't know…" and then she looks away, comforted only by her blank stare at the gray-tiled floor. Looking into nothingness is a barrier for looking into the psyche. No one pressed charges for the death of her grandchild. She was allowed to go, probably because her daughter never wanted to see her again.

Denise secretly thinks about the soul of her grandson. Sometimes she just wants to go and find him. That is the only time she is happy-when she thinks of dying and ending the pain. But because she was raised as a Catholic, she believes she would never see her grandson if she killed herself. So she thinks more about what makes her feel good, and when her check comes from the city, she cashes it and picks up some dope and gets high.

In the bathroom, sitting on a bench in the same intoxicating, tiled room is the beauty whom a special aide calls "baby."

Franny is eighty-seven years old, and still a striking woman. Even with no teeth and a humped back, it is easy to see how beautiful she once was. She has all her hair, and when she lets it down, she looks like a daisy. She smokes like a chimney and is clearly psychotic. Forgetting where she is, she kneels on the bathroom floor and puts her hands together, closes her eyes, and prays to Jesus. She lines up her notes and scribbled-on papers, and one note says: "Do not touch this box of Depends. It belongs to Franny."

Franny urinates on herself, and if there are no diapers in the shelter, she gets very angry and bangs the bench and yells to invisible people. Wearing only black even on bright, warm days, she believes she looks younger in it.

But it is through Franny that the female staff know what their bodies will look like when they are octogenarians. There is hair only on her head. Beautiful, thick gray-and-blond hair. Her tiny white body needs lots of protection. Maintenance men do turnarounds when they catch a glimpse of her when washing bare-assed in the bathroom. She loves to wash in the slop sink. Contradiction: She wouldn't let her male social worker pick out clothes or stay with her to pick out clothes because she is too shy. Yet she washes completely nude with the bathroom door open, hitting the sides of the sink, yelling at herself. She wipes inbetween her legs with peroxide, stands on the Daily News paper, and cries from the burning pain.

When she takes psychotropic drugs that are prescribed by a psychiatrist, she laughs and is quiet. Her writing is less angry. There is no family that we know of for Francis to go and live with. She approaches the reception desk, crying from the pain in her vagina that she doesn't live here. No one is to visit her. She knows they are coming to kill her.

Latonia

Latonia paces the shelter like a dog in a cage. She smokes in the basement as often as she breathes. Without stopping to sit long enough to eat, she rattles around smacking her bags into the air, perhaps at people we cannot see fights when she looks into the mirror at herself. "Mi madre esta muerta," she says, and then spits, "stupido." The maintenance crew hate it when she does that, even worse than pee on the floor, for some reason. Maybe because it's venomous spit as opposed to unintentional peeing.

Latonia has her face smashed up to the elevator door, waiting for it to open. She wants nothing to do with her social worker. She gets off the car and walks up to the wall and tells it off, pointing her finger. She holds onto a travel bag like she is going someplace, always going someplace else. But she never does. At 6:30 a.m. every day, she goes into the traffic and approaches cars for money. It is then that she knows how to smile. How to nicely cajole East-side drivers and taxis into loosening up their wallets.

Today a young woman walked into the shelter to see Latonia. Staff looked long enough to know that it was her daughter. The hairline and an expression around the nose was the same. The visitor went up to Latonia, put her hand on her coat sleeve and said, "Mother?"

Latonia looked at her for a long time. The daughter said: "You look so different. You've changed so much." And then she cried, "Why won't you come home with me? Come on, Mother, please come with me. I want to take care of you."

Latonia shook her head no. "I don't leave here to go there. Here is better for me! Maybe not for you, but es better for me."

The daughter continued to observe the anger and hatred that was on her mother's face. Psychosis is an illness that she could not understand. The daughter believed it was the devil and that the people in the shelter were not helping her mother to get well. Tremendous sadness came over the young woman.

"Just leave with me now and we can get you help, Mother. Please come home with me, I'm asking you this last time, please get your things and come home."

Latonia took a deep breath, her eyes furrowed. She said: "You and Popi tried to take the demons out of me, but I have no demons. The demons are in you and you Popi and I will never go to live in you house. My mother died for you and you knows this to be true. Mi madre es tu Jesus. And I want to bees with Jesus and pray that he takes me each and every days I pray for this."

The daughter stood frozen for a few moments like an arctic tree. "My children need their grandmother, I need my mother and I come here to take you back and this is the way you treat me?" The daughter took out her Bible and started to recite a verse. The mother started to scream at the top of her voice like she was being murdered.

Lana

Dressing up, her face looking pretty, as pretty as she can, Lana lines her eyes with black on the upper and lower lids. Blue powder added for enhancement in the eye socket, she looks almost good, but she never washes her clothes or her hair and in fact wears a knit, red cap on her head all year long, even in the summer. And during that season, she wears the same woolen skirt, worn out with holes on the hipster parts from her arms waving back and forth. She gets angry because of the unnecessary deaths that she believes the shelter is responsible for, and when beef is served two days in a row. "Manager," she yells out, "what is this food doing in this dining room?" She yells at the manager even when the manager is not in the room. "We get $22,000 each year to live off at this shelter and you feed us beef? I would not eat beef on my own, why the hell do you serve it to us?"

Many of the women are at this moment eating what was catered in for the dinner meal. They are quiet and don't want to hear her ranting. Most of them are hungry and glad to have the meal before them. They want her to shut up and to leave the room.

"My husband would never bring a store cooked meal into our home and would turn over in his grave if he knew that they were serving it here, in front of me. He also would not approve of me wearing sneakers. Now, what kind of shoes are these, sneakers are no sort of a shoe. These are cheaply made, over-priced footwear not intended for real ladies."

Lana's front top teeth push out from what a normal bite would be. She drools a bit when spanking the manager with her opinions. Lana wears white stockings with vertical and horizontal rips in them. Her legs look like a nurse's as she

109

changes her clothes. She insists on saving the shredded nylons. Sometimes she sleeps in them. There is something about Lana that makes you want to like her. At times she makes sense and she seems like a friend, then wallop…she's in the faces of the staff, sending them into unplanned sessions with other social workers as they sort out Lana and her illness.

Lana keeps asking the shelter for a sandbox. She says that then the children will come and it would make the shelter a happier place to be. She has been buying sand pails and shovels for them to play with. Sometimes she fills up her water pistol and squirts it at whoever is within her range. She's adamant about the sandbox, and says that when the shelter gets one she will stop squirting the water pistol.

Lana flits around like a bird. A crane, with its long, straight legs and heavier top, then she puts her arms around Cheryl and tells her that she loves her. Too quickly the crane pushes Cheryl away like an unwanted paramour. Staff walk over to her, two at a time, banana cream pie still on their lips, munching on the crust, hittin' and missin' the mission as they compete for kissin' preoccupied, really, with a new staffer.

The day-old woman, Cheryl, just so new on the armory block, talks all about herself. "Now if I wanted to I could buy anything that I want. Do you know that? Anything," she says, expressing herself with a closing snarl. She wiggles her hips and squishes her thighs together when she walks around the small bathroom area. "My mother was a debutante and my father was a military man and I grew up in the elegance of the deep South. We were wanted colored, not like the trash up here in the North. You are just a housekeeper," she says to the manager. "My mother had a shoe shiner who was better bred than you."

Cheryl sees the bathroom as her own, the dorm where her bed is stationed as her room.

#   #   #

There's purple on Feliciana's lips, and a good reason for it being there; she has a disease that comes into the moistness of her mouth every now and then, and she knows that it is there because her father says so, and he never lies. Ever.

There are anklet socks on her feet and the hem on her skirt is always below her knee: just below. Proper, and improperly divorced, this lady, who is of the talkie, chatty kind, could even be your aunt or a cousin in your family, but she lives here at the shelter because she is homeless. She is a sheltered homeless, but still homeless, meaning that, as one other sheltered homeless lady said one day: "We're here because we can't make it out there on our own."

"My daddy rubbed raspberry red on our sores when we was kids and it was some sort of germ that he said us kids had gotten from a dirty can or something. My mom was not too cautious where we was concerned, he was always sayin', but now I think he was right. There are all sorts of things we can catch. That's why I stay away from the other women," Feliciana said, as she crumbled over to the direction of the wall.

Glenna

While washing her clothes, pulling out the knob on the dial of the washing machine that had too many items in it, a spike mouthed woman, Glenna, chose to ignore the stares from the other women on the washing machine waiting list line.

Her two teeth, one on the top, one on the bottom, miss each other when she shuts her mouth, causing her face to look like it's beginning to turn itself inside out. The newest lady in the shelter, Glenna, is the loudest and at this moment the most difficult to discern. The regular loud ladies become quiet. Their eyes get big. They try to walk lightly or stay in one spot so they don't disturb her. The new queen of the blue-chipped bench rules, as she lies down and takes a nap at noon.

Distraction can be an attraction only if it works, but it doesn't work today, even after the aide yells: "Lunch time ladies. They havin' tuna on a bun, cole slaw, beets, juice, and nice, ripe bananas. Now I know you all aren't gonna wait till those bananas are all gone before you catch the elevator to 'three'."

The aide went over to Glenna, "You can't lie here like this. All the other ladies here have no place to sit if you lie down all over the bench the way you are doin'."

Glenna sits up, squints at the figure before her, and says: "See, darling, there is something here that you don't understand. When you get to be as old as I am, it just don't matter no more. You can say whatever the hell it is you gotta say, but it don't matter. I can't move like you want me to move, and I ain't got nowhere to go. So what cha goin' to do?"

"You need to go see a social worker and get yourself a bed pass. Now lets get you to steppin' on up and outta here."

Twelve women are standing aside smoking in the dank, fluorescent-lighted bathroom. Sheena puffs and smokes with the cigarette permanently in her mouth, then puts her head into the cloud of smoke and sniffs it in through her nose. Soap rises up from the source of contempt, all illnesses in the fifth-floor bathroom focus and peak out of their psyches because Glenna went out of turn on the washing machine waiting list line.

Glenna lies back down and closes her eyes. She wears a champagne color beige wig; the stitched line that's supposed to be a part of the wig, falls downward so it is just above her ear. Her belly is exposed when the elastic on her pants falls below her abdomen, pushing softly outward with stretch marks in crystallized rows of fat. Her body is silenced in seconds. Glenna's life has been extended by emergency room doctors. Her body is a patchwork of trauma. Fear keeps this body posted on the same bench until a social worker comes to her side.

"Hi, Glenna. What's going on?"

Glenna opens one of her hairless eyes: "What chu botherin' me for?"

"You can't stay on the bench like this."

"Who say I can't?"

"We have rules, Glenna. Now please sit up."

Glenna is now putting most of her body weight onto her elbow. The wig seems to make sense now that her head is straight. Some stare at it, waiting for it to fall off, others wonder how it is held onto her head. Their eyes spark with light as they stand and wait for Glenna to take her position against the staffer. She rolls off the bench, falling onto her feet, crouched into a bending position. Glenna looks upward...the wig, is her world, is tilted and wrong. It's knotty, and smells sour. Glenna pulls it off her head. "What chu goin to do whit me?" she asks.

"I'm sending you to the basement, and if you continue, we will call the police to escort you out of the building."

"No you ain't."

"Let's go, right now, downstairs."

"My wash…"

"We'll keep it for you in a basket."

Glenna picked up her coat from the bench. She walked slowly, hobbling and bending far to the right with each step. In the elevator, she put her coat on, the wig into place. Once downstairs, she said good-bye to everyone and left the building. Glenna never came back to the shelter again.

Shirley

The corner of the table was the only thing between them. Who was right and who was wrong was lost in the shrieking tenor of verbose female voices. It was Wednesday, and a lot of the staff were out of the building with combined reasons of sick days and meetings. Wednesday was not the day to have a fight. The women floated around the table like sharks targeting a possible meal. They leaned against door frames and put half of their well-cushioned asses on garbage cans. Rarely could they be seen standing alone without any support. A metaphor, perhaps, for how they felt about themselves.

"What do you mean I can't go back inside the shower when the men are done cleaning?"

"That's not what I said," the aide shot back.

"I am allowed to go back inside when they are done. You cannot stop me."

"Shirley, I don't want to stop you, you can go inside now."

"But you told me to get out, and that I couldn't go back into the shower."

"That was when the men were trying to clean it, but they are done now and you can take the shower."

"What do you have against me. I have done nothing to you. All I ever want is to be left alone. I don't bother anyone, I mind my own business. Why don't you answer me, you are supposed to answer me." Shirley pulled her facial features up into the center of her face. She squinted her eyes, pursed her mouth. Her nostrils widened. "I have an appointment today and now I can't even take a shower on time, I can't believe this is happening to me. What have I done to you to deserve this treatment?"

115

Shirley's eyes were black darts against her white, dry skin. She knew the truth. She was always right. She was singular in her thoughts the way one clip held her hair up against the back of her head. The shower she took ownership over was lined with plastic bags across the floor, the entrance and all six hooks on the wall had her plastic bags hanging off them. It had become Shirley's shower. The toilet had become Shirley's toilet, lined and stuffed in the partition openings with plastic bags. The Shirley signature, like designer labels, was established in the women's room.

"And real soon," Shirley continued, "I am going to leave this place and then I am going to go to the Department of Homeless Services and tell them about all the abuse that goes on here at this shelter. They have no idea how cruel you people are to us."

"No one is bothering you now, Shirley, why don't you just go and take care of your business."

"I will go when I damn well feel like it. Who are you to tell me that? I want you to listen to me and I want you to listen real well."

The aide set the Scrabble board up for two players. Flipping over the letters, scrambling them around, he asked who was going to play.

AJ

Then there was AJ. Joanne worked with her. Everyone did! But Joanne was secretly enchanted with her lost eyes. A faraway look of a person who cried even when her eyes were dry. She showed up one morning for work and AJ was there on a bench. AJ talked with the other women like she had known them for a long time. They focused on her as she discussed her life.

Beyond her eyes were her lips that were outlined in green: tattooed lines pointing to a kiss when her mouth was closed. Navy blue lines, permanently etched along the curve of her eyelids. Joanne met with her during the daytime hours, they sat on the benches. Her sadness was real. No tattooed feelings. They wept most of the time. Easy to see when she walked around in the day with the blanket over her eyes. But it was her man who was on her mind, while she curled and braided the hair of the other women who live in the shelter. Adding on hair extensions to the split ends; beginnings of fertilized seeds. Helping each other to grow.

Then the day came when her husband showed up at the shelter door for her. At least one decade younger than she. He waited for her outside the shelter's main exit. He grabbed her by the head, pulling out the Lady Godiva hair, not by the roots, but by the shaft, until her hair was raggedy again and strikingly similar to Ms. Sonia's skirt.

She held her hands up to keep his from hitting her face. Her lipstick would not be worn off; her eye makeup would stay intact. He struck her head with his fist and she cried. She closed her eyes. "No Poppi," she said, crinkling her eyelids until the navy blue tattooed lines disappeared into squinting windows.

117

He doesn't listen to her. He will never hear her words. Instead, he is conjoined with her soul life that waits for her to pay her karmic debt. The husband focuses on her mind, through her tatoo-laced eyes. AJ's tears disappear as soon as they come out, dissolving into her skin, seeping below the epidermis, layering diseases there to form later on into cancer.

She doesn't listen to the social worker who tells her not to give him the address of the shelter. She can only hear the husband: her God who dripped into her white cells, like an intravenous feeder, when she cried.

Joanne immediately missed AJ when she heard that she had left the shelter. Staff wanted to stare at her dreams, to listen to her depression, to learn to understand their own formulas from her stage.

Sonia, in her large filth and chronically rage full personality, could only comment that AJ was full of shit. "The gypsy," Sonia said, "was a liar." No doubt she was envious of AJ's creative beauty against her own beastly charms.

The enchantment with AJ would last for months. The distaste for Sonia was equally established.

#   #   #

At times the shelter staff are guilty. Mostly, they can be found caring for the women, and it comes easily and is a joyful thing to do. A great way to make a living by helping other people get their lives in order. They learn to love each woman for her own glow. Each with a spark from the universe. One that they recognize; one that they share.

Frances has eight black garbage bags filled with her things. Under the bed, along the bed and on top of it, she smothers in clothes and memories that will go to her new home with her.

<u>LOVE</u>

Karen Maxwell

Joanne's lover Eric is still in Colorado. He calls her up once a week to talk dirty to her. She listens, remembering the actual experience. He keeps her flowing this way. They are about sex together. They take their intelligence for granted. He hums around Joanne's mind torturing her soft arena. At thirty-one years old, she is forceful and accomplished to the rest of the world. Two scholarly degrees, and many men later, she has arrived at this women's shelter to impart her experience and to discover her own potential.

After work she jogs two miles. Up and down the city streets, running away from her day, exorcising a life without the phantom man who, on the other end of the phone, excites her into sadness. Every day she wants to get up and cut her emotional losses. Her doctor man, in middle America, calls her during his breaks while he does his residency from the enclosure of the Rocky Mountains. Eager females that he doesn't tell her about distracting his view. She imagines women crawling onto his lap after his twenty-hour shifts end.

And during her days, with the women at the shelter, feeling a pull into their world, their symptoms, just like hers, but theirs with exaggeration. She learns each day that women are basically the same. The women, like all women, stuck in a sphere of a zone in which they breathe the same air, process the same insecurities, try to find love.

They, different from she as they had the chance to fail. She wants the time to do the same. For the world to see her as less stoic. Some days, to melt into the floor, to become a marbleized woman who mixes with all the women, instead of a dictator who guides the lives of others and enforces the rules.

Hold the words, Eric. Bring the lair closer to home. Let her have children through whom she finds her future and rediscovers her past. Give her the turmoil of a family of her own to bring her into the hearts of others from the experience instead of only the instructional.

When Frances looks at Joanne she knows she sees her void. She hasn't had a child, so how can she truly understand the life with one. How can she stop being a schoolgirl in her eyes? In the eyes of others?

Bill, the weekend aide, takes his time with Celeste. Except for her addictions, she is a vibrant woman who dresses like a woman in love. Bill looks away from Celeste with his eyes, yet his body lunges forward from his seat. The pull for them is very strong. This bay of females know how the two of them feel. The gender of the *witch* cannot be fooled. Bill slows up when he talks to her, looks into her face seconds too long; she, right through her olive skin, blushes and glows. Their muscles say that they know each other.

Laughter and small talk. "Is it raining? Are you going to the store? That's so funny." When no one else cares or is laughing.

Homeless ladies in thimbles and cardboard. Beads of pearls; rings in different themes. The devil has visited their minds and left behind tight residue. Staying too long in the hearts of others, lined up with thoughts of the men who've had them siphoning the ego, the id, the consciousness and the soul. Then they are shown the door of another life where dead men lie underneath their beds.

One tells the other that she, will be going to the hospital tomorrow. The other in sunglasses, in the night, keeps a vigil from her bed, kicking her feet to keep away the monster who raped her. Not now, but then, when she was light, and she could walk, and her feet held up her bent legs and curved white spine.

"I want to be," Frances confides, "the woman my mother wanted me to be and the woman that I am supposed to be." This broken soul lies in her bed where the streetlight beams in and warms the face that holds a cold mind. The voids that she needs to own before she can connect her life with fluidity are becoming clearer for her.

Theresa sits up on her bed, winding her hair around her finger until it bleeds. Scrambling along the hallway during the day; eliminating nature from her droll colors. Nothing else can be let in to destroy her view of the world. She hides her face with her hands and giggles. Bad teeth, white with brown stains and large spaces between them, command notice.

A new client takes refuge on the avenue-the city bench in the middle of Park Avenue. She speaks no English and has the belly of a breeder. She had babies and now holds only mystery in her arms as a newcomer to the shelter. Question marks surround her unkempt head of hair. She holds a straw bag with a row of black elephants on it. Nose to tail, they connect all along the exterior of the bag.

"Ola," she says. Joanne watches the curly moist hair that frames her forehead. She looks studious with her unsmiling face. Joanne instantly has respect for her.

"Ola," Joanne responds. She smiles back, grateful perhaps for having been heard. Joanne thinks she is important. She is new here and she wants to make a difference in her life.

The answer is in her eyes. The face keeps them soft. But she can't smile in English. Only in Spanish. Americans tell her to close her eyes and to cry. Not with their words, but with their shoulders and feet and the way they smile at each other and not at her. Americans stop their movements when she walks past them. Brash American women make her fearful; their sense of fun makes her sad.

She avoids the Americans so she doesn't have to hear the answers about her children or her husband. She will be certain, no matter what they say, that it is the Americans fault that she is alone. That her children don't visit her or cry any longer on her breasts. The tiny elephants have become a symbol explaining who she is. Day after day Joanne looks at the elephants: small and strong. Big bellies and swirling tails. This precious, mislocated Latina, in a strange land of people who eat funny and dress in rich and colorful clothes. The Americans throw out food before it turns bad. And she wonders why? Why do they do that?

Tuesday, September 21, 1999

Frances sits back and receives. Her eyes stare into the reasons of why they are here. Her pupils dart at the women in the corners of the hall. She is nearing her time to leave. Separation in the shelter is a task. Similar to watching someone getting ready to jump off a building. Frances ties up the physical ends to her life at the shelter. She is the same as her co-clients and that's the part that scares her. She makes a list of what she will take with her to her new home. Art projects, books, donated clothes, and friendships. The poem she wrote about her buddy Theresa.

Armed, in the stairs, fusing into space,
Theresa wounded in battle, keeps our hearts at a
distance,
Southern picket fence keeps us away.

She re-learns the definition of love: that it also exists in letting go. It can be found in giving others freedom to try life out in their own way.

#   #   #

The shelter paints over paint over paint. Bonds liquid into crevices to seal cracks. Replaces and scrapes floors. Pulls scotch tape off landmark woodwork. Screws in 100-watt light bulbs into 60-year-old lights. Dumps water buckets, deodorizes beds, sanitizes floors, plunges shit and paper down toilets with narrow drains, pulls soup cans that are used as spittoons out of the sewage starting point.

The shelter workers unconsciously adopt the women into the weave. They see what they do, even when they think they aren't looking. Trailing through the floors, afire with their personal missions, each woman's agenda is transparent for their good.

They clean refrigerators, catch mice, spray the flies and arrest the eggs. The elevator is the most used cavity in the shelter. They test their own abilities to care. They teach society's lepers to love themselves. They hope they learn.

Frances recalls the Vietnam war to Joanne. It was a jungle, even in America. Free love cost her a father for her child. The love for him stayed in her like an ice cube that got stuck in the back of her throat. She couldn't swallow without pain. Sex became a thought with a memory attached to it. Afraid to love ever again. The abdomen was too fat, breasts too low, lips tight and dull. The only life she remembered was when she was twenty years old and living like a car in fourth gear without the wheels ever touching the ground.

Yet her mind played tricks on her and every once in a while the smell of *Tabu* came along, or a *Beetles* song. Only then did the desire come, with the recall of sex with Donald on the couch in his basement in 1969. New suede boots drying out under the heater before his mother came home from work. A recall of the boots shriveling up with snow stains throws her back into the present, zap into the shelter dorm with key to her locker looping around her neck. New keys to the SRO she will soon inhabit in her hand; where did everything go? The war for the homeless feels like Vietnam all over again. They loose. They win. Power. No power. The poor are always the losers. The new poor are powerless all over again. Disenfranchised from their families, the plastic backs of the shelter chair, holding them up, securing them to the shelter floor, become the love in their lives. Holding up dried-out disco women with osteoporosis. Shocked with their mental illnesses to take cover in the new foreign land of the shelter. One hundred and nineteen lovers, and children recalling Christmas time from the annual one-gift holiday season.

Meals are puffed with gravy and coffee excites them into fast walks in the halls and to their youth. Some go outside for sterno heated meals from the Korean deli or oil mixed salads for $3.99 a pound.

Love revisited when they collapse on their beds. Dreaming toward the 40-foot-ceiling and seeing love in the now. Dazed, spent faces for a moment, bland as they journey backward in time, then abandon the present in their sleep.

The fat lady falls onto her bed. A deep sigh rises from her breath. Silence in the dorm at three o'clock. They are in love with sleep. The windows with half daylight shadows triangle across the panes where Sheena sees Jesus. "I love you," she says.

Sigrid walks in. An unlit cigarette bounces off her lip. Mandy's bed is piled high with things shaped into a block form. Impacted like an intestine.

Herminia rubs her hands together. Her large white teeth stark against her tan face, she's happy to see Joanne. Squinting her eyes in excitement, so happy to see the night aides. In love with the shelter, she feels good, as the shelter food was satisfying.

The staff, in overview, wait for the meds to kick in to quiet the erratic. Walls ensconced with bodies that speak in many languages and chatter to one another in mirrors. Our once-friendly maidens who once upon a time saw the world in their lovers, eyes. The feminine demon, age, crept up and stabbed them in their backs. After all those years of seducing partners for meals and demanding through their beauty that their bills be paid and their children be fed, they got old. Felt ugly. Were lost. Called crazy. How could that be?

Earning the vision that each woman foresaw, fading love naturally followed their fading looks. Fair only for the Pentecostal, and pious Herminia who found Jesus. Dressing like a nun who left her vows: long navy blue skirt, white blouse, faded-creamy beige underwear, hair in a net, and the precious gold cross overlapping the top button on her blouse. Herminia refuses to dance with the radio.

Carve the lady out of the wood. She is bonded into it, the artisan can't leave the shelter. They can't chisel her out. She's molded into the door frame, waiting to unmask her canvases and paint her bold strokes onto the primed surface. Yet she is unable to live outside of the shelter and can only cram her locker and under her bed with paints and water bottles for the mix. Her face is thrown into her hands. Someone knocks on the door in her mind. She bangs her fists into the air. She blinks her eyes and points her finger, "Get away," she says.

Dr. Delaney blesses the walls where her bed borders the head by Frances's foot and the foot of her bed toward the emergency door. She's eating peach cobbler from a Harlem restaurant that she visits when her check comes in, and twice a month the sugar sends the knuckles on her hands into redness from food sensitivity. A palm cross is tied into the metal bed frame with wire.

She says to a partial audience of other women, "Men are a different breed. I just wanted him to know that even though he was good for a man, he just wasn't good enough for me!"

The world outside the shelter culture sees rags on a human form scraping along the sidewalk on a New York City street. They don't know that the shelter ladies are happy for fences and trees that they can grab onto here and there for support. Rhythms of the Islands, of the 1950s and 60s bang and pound in their heads. The shelter staff know the personas are silly.

Babbling women who in tick formation reveal their lonely lives. A mirror crops up for the other people who have homes and apartments. There, but for the splendor of the universe, they are. Look at me, the homeless women scream with their slow walks and unsightly smells. I am you! I am your mother! I am your child! Don't look at me and I will still be here. I have nowhere else to go. Everyone seems to be feeding off of them. A definition of what is the worst place to be: homeless. The sadness in their eyes always on your mind when you look into the mirror and see you!

Dr. Delaney keeps the love in her life. A dorm mate sits and listens as she remembers: "And then a wave comes over me and there it is. All over again. I remember the school in Chinatown and the smell of chicken base in the heat. A small wind passed over our espresso as we sat on fine, white-leather strips in the chairs on the street. On Sundays, on Mondays. I could have that man, his name was Cali, any day, but the *where* was the problem, 'cause we were homeless together.

"We made love behind a box on Barrow Street on an October morning. We was up all night long and we was just talking and then we did it just naturally.

"But all the papers I had of us and pictures was lost in another shelter. But I got these pictures in my mind and no one can take them away from me. No one can take the love that that man and I shared together, even if it was on the streets in Greenwich Village."

#   #   #

The maintenance men are clearing out AJ's locker. Dumping her hair, for weaving long, waist-length braids and nail polish bottles in green and black, hardened and crusted on the outside in drips. Each stroke, during a day of

129

quiet with the other maidens, now dead to the shelter society as it now exists. Frances mourns AJ's departure and looks away as the staff drop the cosmetics into the garbage bags.

AJ gave it up for love. Defined by the time she was ten years old as a battlefield that she had to swing her arms from side to side to defend for, and against, in her life. Love, the image forecasted into her psyche from magazine covers. The most important thing in her life she could not learn. She cried for forgiveness from her man when she did nothing wrong. AJ pursued men who had hard hands and black eyes. Rage in the bed was fulfilling. Then she felt alive and she could call her mother and sisters and tell them how Manuel beat her. They would listen in earnest, each punch and bruise a reminder of how much he cared for her. Encouraging her to stay with him, that he really loved her, and that he would change, eventually. "They all do."

Donita throws open her locker to embrace her image in the mirror on the door. She combs her hair as she bends over. From the bottom of the scalp to the front, the gray-and-blond hair flies like a horse's tail. She glosses her lips, pouting her lips there to the image.

Lana sits on her made bed. Lana's covers are not shelter provided, but a floral-and-grass print from the life she had with her husband. The husband who wouldn't let her eat meat. Who frowned at sneakers. The man who ran away with a beautiful young African American princess one Friday afternoon, while Lana played Sarah Vaughn songs from the 1960s. She was cooking a pot roast with carrots and potatoes for the evening meal. It got darker and darker into the evening and her man called to tell her that he wasn't coming home again.

She stopped cooking and washing, and smoked catatonically in her house until she was evicted. No man, no money. Lana became more catatonic in the days and the months that folded and sealed during the years that she was sheltered. She fell in love with cigarettes and beautifully made beds with neat, full pillows and tightly tucked sheets in the corners.

Big Andrea wears sunglasses, as someone stole her makeup bag and she won't let anyone see her this way. Puffed "Mommy" eyes and sallow, loose skin are not the way to look if you want to get love. Pretty that face up, my Momma. Keep it in a tube. Hold the feelings in, let the appetite speak for you. There is nothing to hide from the rest of the world. But your silence and sunglasses tell all.

Lynn finds love in a bottle of vodka. A twin to Sigrid, yet they don't see it in themselves. The other has the drinking problem: not she. A potion to hit the central nervous system where love is numbed into the belief that not having it doesn't matter. The magic that helps the world feel good. Limiting what she hears, what she sees.

Sheena, our swinging Lady of the Jungle, ripens her fruits in the canvas bag that was given to the women during a volunteer day. Sweet balls of peaches, and apples turning soft from age, the way her mother would ripen fruits when she was a child. The love of a dead son keeps Sheena from abandoning the shelter life. As the only life that she wants after the shelter is the afterlife. She writes notes in journal books and recognizes great writers from the content of their material. A connoisseur of refinement, this reader digests the *Wall Street Journal* on a daily basis, and argues worldly issues, in between the voices in her mind.

"Yes I know," she will say. And the staff know that she is communicating with the people in there, in her head. Maybe with the son who is on the other side, telling her to leave the weave of the shelter life.

Betti, our Jamaican Queen, so quiet and mournful. Dementia in the Alzheimer's state. "Are you my baby?"

she says to Chynna Maryanne. Without waiting for an answer, Betti wraps her pissed-up coat around Chynna Maryanne's shoulders. It is a sopping wet wool red coat that drips of piss when it is picked up. "Here, baby, please, thank you baby. You wear this now for Mommy is going to the store now and will return real soon."

Chynna Maryanne shudders the coat to the floor. Her blue-chiffon, flowing puffy clothes are threatened with filth. Her body is now dirty. She runs, her slippers kicking up dust, into the closest shower. The smell makes her throw up. Water seeps through her eyes. She went into the dorm to dream about the babies. Believing that today she would be able to grab one and hold on to it, like the daughter she had in Cuba.

Chynna Maryanne thinks that the devil has come to her through Betti. He now takes control over her because of all the terrible things that she has done in her life. The water washes over her chilled body and she makes the sign of the cross to Jesus and asks for his forgiveness. She is too dirty to pray. Her mind is filled with ideas of where to take her baby, who is waiting outside for her in a stroller. The pretty baby with a yellow hat and white shoes. The infant girl with black hair, yes. The baby in her mind is hers, and it is okay. And when she sees it, they will both know that she is the mother.

But the red coat with pee is in her face and she throws up again in the shower. She curls into the wall and cries. The women hear her and they wait for her to come out of the water, past the shower curtain, so they can comfort her.

Ava holds open a towel and rolls it over Chynna Maryanne's back. Ava sees the holes in the walls and yells at staff to cover them. To take away the knives, to put back the metal detector. "Don't you see what is happening here? This poor woman is traumatized and no one is doing anything about it."

Wednesday, September 22, 1999

The Last Hours

"I want to blame someone," Frances begins. "I want to get angry at my mother, my father. I'm fifty-six years old and tired. I should have a home and a steady job. I should be piling up money for retirement right now, instead of leaving a homeless shelter for one room."

"Homelessness can happen to anyone," Joanne tells her. "There are no rules in life for when one should be in need."

"But I also feel good, it's so complicated. This is so exhilarating, and so embarrassing. I want to fly out of the cage, and I want to stay. I want to die here in darkness like Theresa will. Sometimes I think it's easier just to stop living. Let others do it for me. I can call my daughter now. She can call me. I can let her in again."

Joanne smiles. She waits for Frances to say more. The therapy is in motion all the time in this place. It's the happenings in an instant that prove to be more helpful than the planned sessions. The spontaneity gives her ownership of the change. Removing the social worker, in the parental role, from her growth.

She continues, "I don't hear voices like a lot of the women here do, but something deep inside always felt a bit disconnected. Like I was going through the actions and motions of living like everyone else. My whole life I felt like I couldn't breathe. And I believed that if I stopped and tried to breathe, that everything I was holding together would fall apart. If I were rich I wouldn't have lost my home. But I am poor, like all the other women who can't stop spinning and spinning."

Yes, Joanne thought, the givers and the holder-uppers. That's what women are. "You are young enough to start over. You are healthy and educated. You've kept good habits throughout your life and now you can reap the rewards for your future."

Closure. The word is used, but people don't really put closure on important things. They close doors, but can never put closure on feelings. That's where their hearts are, but they can put them to rest, so the honest way for Joanne to approach Frances was to tell her that. How could there be closure for her and what had taken place in her life? She was moving on and moving well, but there would only be perhaps a partial closure, as Joanne was always going to be there for her. Even if she didn't come back, it didn't matter. In her mind, it must remain open. The vision she needs to have of this experience is that Joanne will always remember her and that she was always important to her. The women she had lived with would be celebrated in her heart for the rest of her life.

The women line the large hall in spotted areas. A long line of safety against the walls. They bargain for mental illness in a healthy way. The ones left behind, as Frances moves on, are going holistic with their mental illnesses. No one is going to medicate them. There is comfort and familiarity with the voices in their heads, and the visions of others who they believed were out to get them. The fits of rage can mean that lots of people were coming to their aid. When love is found this way it is hard to give up.

Theresa claps her hands together, rubs the palms fast, happy with the friction. Her toothless smile is broad and she has abandoned concern about how she looks without teeth.

Joanne is consumed with her today. She visits the hall where Theresa sleeps and plays during the day and night. Where she meets with the dead in her family, the etched figures in the chipped walls.

The handyman's voice echoes from the bathroom to the hall. Sounds like a Spanish wedding. Not easy to discern whether they are talking about the new shower heads or the dinner they had last night. Theresa and Joanne smile briefly at the volume from the men over the running water.

"Feel my hands," Theresa says. "I am so cold."

Joanne reaches over and touches her. She feels like stone. Today her scarf is white and she is wrapped up in a white sheet. She shivers and now has fear in her eyes. Joanne thanks God that she knows her. Theresa's body is shaking from the terror from the loss of Frances. Reliving the loss of her kin when she was thrown out of her father's house decades ago.

"We are not going to throw you out," Joanne says. "We are not going to throw you out the door onto the street with nowhere to go."

The day will come when one of them will leave this place. They are like partners in Theresa's life. Co-leaders for a broken vessel.

Theresa's Jupiter, Joanne is the sun. Light bulbs brighten up the northern hemisphere of Theresa's head. The western side is dull, and darkened by the direction she is sitting in. She rests her arm on the back of the chair. For months she was combative, and unlovingly watched the staff while they set up supplies and readjusted the post-breakfast energy into the afternoon life of groups and social-worker interventions.

Theresa adopted the staff and her roommates into the memory of her family structure. Most times living the family dynamic all over again, and more recently amending the mistakes. Learning from the staff that they will love her no matter who she talks to in her head, how she dresses, or where she sleeps.

# # #

Frances's bags are on the cart. Eight-large black garbage bags containing the nine month shelter life that she lived in the great fortress of an armory. She is in the bathroom, putting makeup on her face. New colors of pink lipstick and blue pencil for her eyes. The focus is now off the move and has progressed toward her working on a newly established Frances. A Frances who can take care of herself. A Frances who can now look forward to seeing her daughter once again, and maybe she will return to teaching.

Perhaps Frances will cry tomorrow, long after the taxi has left with her new life in it. Today, she officially returns to the adult stage of being a woman. Signing a lease, paying money for her rent, deciding where she wants to work. No longer stuck in the undeveloped stage of dependency and neediness.

Joanne has a love for Frances that is not quite like a friend or a family member. But it's a love in which she, too, was shown that each person is an individual with different needs than anyone else.

Joanne hopes Frances makes it out there. She hopes she never sees her again.

About the Author

Karen Maxwell has been writing poetry since she was a child. She has been published in numerous literary journals and was a reporter in the 1980's for a health tabloid in New York City. She is currently writing two other books. One is about the genocide of the American Indians on Long Island, and the other is on the passion and pain of love.

She grew up in Long Island, New York and currently lives in New York City.